THE PIGGY BANK SOCIETY

PERSONAL FINANCE SIMPLIFIED

THE PIGGY BANK SOCIETY

PERSONAL FINANCE SIMPLIFIED

CHARITH APPACHU

THE PIGGY BANK SOCIETY

PERSONAL FINANCE SIMPLIFIED

CHARITH APPACHU

Table of Contents

Introduction

Welcome to
The Piggy Bank Society

Some kids love sports. Some kids love video games. And others like the ones in *The Piggy Bank Society* love something a little different: *discovering how the world works, one topic at a time.* But don't get the wrong idea. They are not just bookworms buried in research all day. They are also a fun bunch who love cracking jokes, debating big ideas, and occasionally competing to see who can solve a tricky problem first.

———————————◆———————————

Meet *The Piggy Bank Society* - a group of curious 10 to 14-year-olds who have made it their mission to explore the most fascinating topics they can find. They don't just read but they investigate, discuss, and challenge each other to think bigger. Their secret hideout? A cozy corner in the school library, where they gather every week to dive into a new subject. Their goal? To take complicated ideas and break them down into stories that make sense to everyone.

This time, their focus is *money*. What is it, really? Just some numbers on a screen? Pieces of paper and metal? Or is there something much bigger behind it? The Piggy Bank Society is about to find out, and you're invited to join them.

———— ✦◆✦ ————

As you flip through these pages, you will get to sit in on their conversations, hear their discoveries, and take part in their challenges. They'll explore history, science, and psychology, uncovering the hidden truths behind how money works and why saving is a superpower. And the best part is that it is never boring.

———— ✦◆✦ ————

So, are you ready to think like a Piggy Bank Society member? Buckle up! Because this is going to be a fun and eye-opening ride into the world of money, savings, and the smart habits that can set you up for life. Let's get started.

———— ✦◆✦ ————

SEASON 1

FROM BARTER TO BITCOIN

Chapter 1

When There Was No Money

The library felt extra quiet that day. The Piggy Bank Society had gathered again, huddled around their usual table. Aarav dropped a small bag on the table with a clinking sound.

"Guess what's inside?" he asked, grinning.

Zara opened it and pulled out... stones? Shiny ones, some smooth, some odd-shaped.

"Gems?" Kabir asked.

"Sort of" Aarav said. "These are what my granddad called **'trade stones'.** In his village, long ago, people used them to trade before they had proper coins".

"That's exactly what we're going to talk about today" said Ananya. "A time when money, as we know it, didn't even exist".

"Let's go way back" added Rohan. "To when money wasn't metal, paper, or digital. But things".

Before coins and cash, trust was the currency. Barter taught us the first rule of money (i.e) value lies in what you give and what you get

Barter: Trading Without Money

Ananya drew two stick figures on the board.

"One has wheat. The other has fish. They want to trade. That's called **barter**".

"It sounds simple" Kabir said. "You give me what I need, I give you what you want".

"But it had a problem" said Zara. "What if I have apples but you don't want apples?"

"That's called the **double coincidence of wants**" said Rohan. "You both need to want what the other has. Otherwise, no deal".

"So people started using things that everyone found useful" Aarav added. "Salt, shells, cattle, metal objects. These became the *first mediums of exchange*".

Early Forms of Money
Around the World

"*Cowrie shells were used in India*" Ananya said, holding up a picture. "They were shiny, rare, and small. Perfect for trade".

"In Africa, salt blocks were money" said Zara. "That's where the word *'salary' comes from : Salarium - Payment in salt*".

"Native Americans used beads. Romans used metal rods" added Rohan. "Money was always about what people agreed had value".

"Even in Tamil Nadu, people used gold coins and called them *'Kasu'*" Aarav said. "Which is still slang for money today".

"So money was born out of trade" Kabir said. "But it didn't look anything like what we have now".

Why Did People Move Beyond Barter?

"Barter worked when people lived in small groups" said Ananya. "But when societies grew, it became hard".

Rohan listed a few problems:
- *Difficult to carry things around*
- *No way to measure exact value*
- *No system to save or store value over time*

"Imagine trading ten chickens for one goat" Kabir said. "How would you carry them? What if the goat runs away?"

Everyone laughed.

"That's why people started using standardised money. Items that were easy to carry, count, and trust" said Zara.

"And this set the stage for the first real coins" said Aarav.

Quick Recap

Before leaving, Ananya summarised:
- Barter was the earliest way of trading goods and services
- It required both parties to want what the other had
- Early money was based on useful or rare items like salt, shells, and cattle
- Money became more organised as societies grew

"Money didn't just appear one day" Rohan said. "It evolved from what people trusted and found valuable".

"And we're just getting started" Zara added. "Next time, we meet the first coins and paper money. And see how rulers turned trust into currency".

The Piggy Bank Society packed their bags, eyes full of curiosity. They had started a journey that would span thousands of years, across empires, oceans, and technologies. And it had all begun with a bag of stones.

Chapter 2

The Birth of Coins and Paper Money

The following week, the Piggy Bank Society walked into the library with a bit of excitement. Kabir had brought something special.

"Look what I found in my grandfather's trunk" he said, unwrapping a small pouch.

Inside were old metal coins. One was thick and square. Another had a hole in the middle.

"Whoa" said Aarav. "These look ancient".

"They are" said Kabir. "He said one of them is from a time when kings ruled and there were no banks".

"That's perfect" said Zara. "Because today, we're talking about the birth of coins and paper money".

Before wallets had zippers, they had weight. Coins clinked, notes crinkled and the idea of money was born

Why Coins?

"Last time, we saw how barter had problems" said Ananya. "So people started using metals. They were durable, divisible, and easy to carry".

"Metals like gold, silver, copper, and bronze" Rohan added. "And they had real value too".

"Eventually, rulers started stamping their faces or symbols on them" Zara explained. "That's how coins became official money".

In India, the Mahajanapadas used punch-marked coins over 2,000 years ago," said Aarav. "Each mark showed trust from a kingdom or merchant guild".

"And that built confidence" said Ananya. "People accepted coins because they trusted the issuer".

Coins Around the World

Ananya pulled out a chart:

- *China used knife and spade-shaped coins*
- *Greece had coins with images of gods and animals*
- *Rome issued coins to pay soldiers and build roads*
- *India minted coins from silver and copper long before Europe*

"Coins told stories" said Rohan. "About leaders, battles, and trade".

"Even today, you can tell a lot from the coins of a country" Kabir said, flipping one over.

When Paper Replaced Metal

"But carrying lots of coins was heavy" Zara said. *"So in China, around 1,000 years ago, the first paper money was introduced"*.

"It started as **deposit slips**" Ananya explained. "Traders kept coins in a safe place and got a note saying how much they had".

"These notes were later accepted as money" said Rohan. "Because people trusted the place that issued them".

"In India, people used something called **'hundis'**" Aarav added. "Paper notes written by merchants that acted like cheques".

"So paper money was born from the idea of trust and convenience" said Kabir. "Just like coins".

Who Controls the Money?

"Coins were first issued by kings" said Ananya. "Then governments and central banks took over".

"In India today, only the *Reserve Bank of India can print notes*" Rohan explained. "It also decides the designs and denominations".

"And each note carries a promise" Zara said. *"Signed by the RBI governor. It says the note is legal tender and accepted everywhere".*

"That's the power of trust again" said Aarav. "We accept a piece of paper because we believe in the system behind it".

Quick Recap

Zara wrapped up with the key points:
- Coins solved the problems of barter and were backed by trusted rulers
- Different regions created coins in unique shapes and styles
- Paper money began as receipts for stored coins
- India had its own version through
- Today's currency is built on trust in the issuing authority

"Money isn't just metal or paper" said Ananya. "It's a symbol of shared belief".

The Piggy Bank Society packed up, their imaginations full of swords, coins, and promises on paper. History had never felt more real or more valuable.

Chapter 3

The Rise of Banks and Modern Currency

The next meeting began with Zara carrying a bulky old ledger.

"My grandfather used to work at a bank" she said. "This is what they used before computers. Handwritten entries for every deposit and withdrawal".

"Looks like it weighs more than a school bag" joked Kabir.

"But it holds stories" said Zara. "Of how money started living in banks instead of our pockets".

Ananya clapped her hands. "That's perfect. Because today, we're talking about how banks and currency evolved together".

Why Banks Came Into the Picture

"Earlier, people stored their wealth in homes or with trusted traders" Rohan explained. "But it was risky. Theft, fire, loss - no safety".

Banks brought more than money; they brought trust, tracking, and a place for every rupee to feel safe

"*Temples and merchants in ancient India started offering storage*" said Ananya. "They wrote down how much you deposited".

"These paper records became the start of bank-like systems" Aarav added.

"Over time, actual banks were created" Zara said. "To keep money safe and to help it move".

Cheques, Notes, and Promissory Papers

"Banks offered another solution" said Rohan. "Instead of carrying coins, you could write a cheque".

"*You give someone a paper that tells the bank to give them money*" Ananya added. "It was safer and easier".

"And then came **promissory notes**" said Zara. "*Written promises to pay someone a certain amount on a certain date*".

"Sounds a lot like our modern notes" said Kabir. "Only now they're printed by the government".

India's Journey to Modern Currency

"India's currency was a mix of regional coins and foreign influences" said Ananya.

"The British set up the Bank of Bengal in 1806" Rohan added. "It started issuing paper notes".

"Later came the Presidency Banks - Bombay and Madras" said Aarav.

"They merged to form the Imperial Bank of India".

"In 1935, **the Reserve Bank of India (RBI)** was created" said Zara. "It became the sole authority to issue money in India".

"And in 1955, the *Imperial Bank became State Bank of India* - India's biggest public bank" Ananya concluded.

Currency Gets Smarter

"Currency evolved not just in look, but in features" said Rohan. "Security threads, watermarks, serial numbers-all to stop fakes".

"And each note has a value printed on it" said Kabir. "But its true value comes from trust in the RBI".

"Also, each note has a hidden message" said Zara. "Turn it over. It says: 'I promise to pay the bearer the sum of...' signed by the Governor".

"That's a legal promise" said Ananya. "It shows that money is not just paper. It's backed by the country's trust and economy".

Quick Recap

Before leaving, Rohan summed it up:

- Banks were created to store and move money safely
- Cheques and notes replaced heavy coins
- Promissory papers became the early version of currency
- The RBI became India's money authority in 1935
- Modern notes carry trust, value, and security

"Money moved from your hand to your bank" said Aarav. "But the value stayed the same-it's all about trust".

The Piggy Bank Society packed up, their minds buzzing with the realisation that money was not just stored in banks. It grew, flowed, and carried a promise-every single time it changed hands.

Chapter 4

The Digital Shift Begins

It was raining outside, but that didn't stop the Piggy Bank Society from gathering in the library. Aarav shook water off his bag and pulled out a shiny plastic card.

"My mom just gave me an add-on debit card" he said proudly. "I used it to buy books online".

"Welcome to the world of digital money" said Ananya.

Kabir looked confused. "But it's just a card. Where's the money?"

Zara smiled. "That's what we're going to explore today. How money became invisible".

The Age of Plastic

"After paper money came plastic money" said Rohan. **"Debit cards and credit cards changed the way we spend"**.

Money may look different, but its job is the same, helping us move value from one hand to another. Technology just makes the handshake faster

Ananya held up two cards. *"A debit card takes money directly from your account. A credit card lets you borrow and pay later"*.

"And cards are accepted almost everywhere" Zara added. "Shops, online stores, even food delivery apps".

"They also made shopping faster" said Kabir. "No need to count notes or wait for change".

The Magic of ATMs

Rohan showed a photo of an old ATM. *"The Automated Teller Machine was a big step. It lets you withdraw cash without visiting the bank"*.

"In India, the first ATM came in 1987" said Aarav. "Today, there are over two lakh ATMs across the country".

"People could access their money anytime" said Zara. "And that gave them more control".

"Unless you forget your PIN" joked Kabir.

Internet Banking Changes Everything

"Then came net banking" said Ananya.

"People could transfer money, check balances, pay bills - all from home".

"It started slowly in the late 1990s" said Rohan. "But really took off after smartphones became common".

"Banks launched mobile apps. You didn't even need a computer anymore" Zara added.

"Even parents started using it" said Kabir. "My dad pays the electricity bill online now".

Rise of Digital Wallets

"Apps like Paytm, PhonePe, and Google Pay made money even more digital" said Aarav. "You load money in the app and pay with a tap".

"It's especially useful for small shops and street vendors" said Zara. "They don't need a card machine. Just a QR code".

"Digital wallets helped during the 2016 demonetisation too" said Ananya. "When cash was short, people went digital".

But Is It Safe?

"Digital is fast and easy" said Rohan. "But it comes with risks".

Zara listed a few safety tips:
- *Use strong passwords*
- *Don't share OTPs*
- *Avoid suspicious links or fake apps*

"And always double-check the recipient before sending money" said Ananya. "Once it's gone, it's hard to get back".

Quick Recap

Before they packed up, Zara summarised:

- Debit and credit cards made payments faster and easier
- ATMs gave people access to cash 24x7
- Net banking brought banking to your fingertips
- Digital wallets turned phones into money tools
- But with great speed comes the need for caution

"Money is no longer just paper or coin" said Rohan. "It's numbers on a screen".

The Piggy Bank Society packed their bags, realising that the world of money was shifting. And they were moving with it.

Chapter 5

UPI and the Indian Payments Revolution

The Piggy Bank Society met after school in the computer lab this time. Ananya was already logged into a website showing live UPI transaction numbers.

"Look at that" she said. "Over ten billion UPI transactions this month alone".

"Ten billion?" Kabir gasped. "That's more than the total population of the planet".

"Exactly" said Zara. "India isn't just catching up. We're leading the way".

What Is UPI?

Rohan wrote it clearly on the board: **UPI = Unified Payments Interface.**

"It's a system that allows you to transfer money instantly between bank accounts using just a phone" he explained.

*With UPI, India didn't just catch up but it raced ahead.
No cards, no cash, just trust, tech, and a tap*

"No IFSC codes. No account numbers" added Aarav. **"Just a UPI ID or a QR code"**.

"And it works 24x7" said Ananya. "Even at 2 a.m".

How Did UPI Begin?

"UPI was launched in 2016 by the *National Payments Corporation of India (NPCI)*" said Zara.

"It was built to make money movement easier, cheaper, and faster for everyone" added Rohan.

"Even before that, India had digital payments, but they were slow or clunky" said Ananya. "UPI changed the game".

"Now it's built into apps like PhonePe, Google Pay, Paytm, and BHIM" Aarav said.

Why UPI Works So Well in India

Kabir raised a hand. "Why didn't other countries do this first?"

"Good question" said Ananya. "UPI works well in India because of a few big reasons".

She listed them out:

- *Bank accounts linked with Aadhaar and mobile numbers*
- *NPCI created a shared platform for all banks*
- *QR codes made it easy for even small vendors to accept money*
- *No transaction charges for most users*

"India skipped the credit card era and jumped straight into mobile payments" Zara added.

"And we had a strong push from the government after demonetisation in 2016" said Rohan.

UPI in Daily Life

The group took turns describing how they use UPI.

"I use it to split the bill after pizza" said Kabir.

"My mom pays the house help through UPI" said Zara.

"We even paid our exam fees through UPI" Aarav added.

From pani puri stalls to petrol pumps, everyone accepts it" said Ananya. "It's become a habit".

UPI Goes Global

"Did you know India is now exporting UPI to other countries?" Rohan said.

"Like **Singapore and UAE**" said Zara. "They've started accepting Indian UPI apps".

"NPCI is also helping other countries build their own systems" Ananya added. "It's a global success story".

Is There a Catch?

"UPI is great" Aarav said. "But is there a downside?"

"Like all tech, it has risks" Ananya replied.

Rohan listed them:
- *Fake QR codes or scam links*
- *People pretending to be customer support*
- *Sending money to the wrong person by mistake*

"But most of these can be avoided with awareness" Zara said. "UPI is safe if you stay alert".

Quick Recap

Before wrapping up, Ananya summed it all up:

- UPI allows instant bank transfers using just a phone
- Launched by NPCI in 2016, it revolutionised Indian payments
- Works round the clock, with no extra cost
- Widely accepted across India and now growing globally
- Stay alert to avoid scams

"India went from cash-heavy to cash-lite in just a few years" said Rohan.

"And now we're showing the world how it's done" said Zara.

The Piggy Bank Society packed up their things, inspired. The future wasn't coming - it was already in their pockets.

Chapter 6

Psychology of Spending – Why Swiping Feels Easier

The library was unusually quiet when the Piggy Bank Society gathered that day. Kabir looked up from his phone and said, "I just bought a pair of headphones online. Didn't even realise I spent ₹1,200. It felt like clicking a button".

"That's exactly what we're going to talk about today" said Zara. "Why spending digital money feels easier, and sometimes more dangerous".

"It's like the money isn't real" Aarav added.

"But it is" said Ananya. "Your brain just reacts to it differently".

Swiping vs. Handing Over Cash

Rohan picked up a ₹500 note and waved it. "When you give someone this, you physically feel the money leaving".

Cash makes you pause. Cards make you glide. The way we spend changes how we feel and that's the trick your wallet never tells you

"But when you swipe a card or scan a QR code, nothing really leaves your hand" said Zara.

"It's called **pain of paying**" explained Ananya. "It's a real thing. *Studies show that people feel less pain when they use cards or digital payments compared to cash*".

"That's why it's easier to overspend online" Rohan added.

The Role of Dopamine

Zara drew a brain on the whiteboard and circled a small area.

"This is where *dopamine* lives" she said.

"It's a chemical that makes you feel excited or rewarded".

"Like when you get a like on your post or score a goal" said Kabir.

"Exactly" said Zara. "Buying things, especially on sale, gives your brain a quick dopamine hit. That's why shopping feels good".

"But the feeling fades, and we go looking for the next thing" Ananya added. "It's a cycle".

"So basically, shopping is tricking our brains?" Aarav asked.

"In some ways, yes" said Rohan.

Invisible Money = Invisible Budgets

"When we use cash, we know how much we have left" Ananya said.

"But with cards or UPI, we don't feel the pinch until we check our balance" said Zara.

"That's why budgeting is more important now" Rohan added.

Kabir nodded. "I once spent almost my whole allowance on food deliveries in just five days. Didn't realise until I had ₹20 left".

"Exactly the point" said Ananya. "Digital makes spending easier, but saving harder".

Tricks Used by Apps and Websites

"Ever seen those countdown timers on shopping apps?" Zara asked. "Or messages like 'Only 2 left in stock'?"

"Those are psychological tricks" said Ananya. "They create urgency and **FOMO - fear of missing out**".

"And offers like 'Buy now, pay later' or 'No-cost EMI'?" said Aarav. "Those make spending feel safer than it really is".

"It's important to pause and ask: do I really need this?" Rohan said.

How to Outsmart the Urge

Ananya listed a few tips on the board:
- *Wait 24 hours before making a big purchase*
- *Use budgeting apps or notebooks to track spending*
- *Set a weekly spending limit for UPI or card use*
- *Stick to shopping lists*
- *Remove saved cards from shopping apps*

"These small steps help you stay in control" said Zara. "Because the goal is not to stop spending, but to spend smart".

Quick Recap

Before they wrapped up, Rohan summarised:
- *Digital payments reduce the pain of paying, leading to overspending*

- *Dopamine makes us feel good about buying, but only for a while*
- *Online offers play with our emotions*
- *Budgeting is more important than ever in the digital age*

"Money is more invisible now" said Aarav. "But the impact of spending is very real".

"And that's why being aware matters" said Ananya. "You can enjoy your money without losing control of it".

The Piggy Bank Society packed up, each one secretly thinking about the last thing they bought online. Maybe next time, they would think twice before clicking "Buy Now".

Chapter 7

What Is Cryptocurrency? Is It Even Real Money?

The next meeting started with Aarav pulling out a printout of a chart.

"Guys, Bitcoin's price went up again" he said. "But I still don't get how something that doesn't exist physically is worth so much".

"That's the mystery of crypto" said Zara. "And today, we're going to decode it".

Ananya smiled. "Welcome to the wild world of cryptocurrency".

What Is Cryptocurrency?

Rohan wrote the word on the board and broke it down.

"'Crypto' means hidden. 'Currency' means money. So, cryptocurrency is digital money that's secured by codes and math".

Not all money jingles in your pocket. Some just zips through the internet - invisible, yet real in a whole new way

"It's not printed by any government" added Ananya. "It lives entirely online".

"And the most famous one is **Bitcoin**" said Kabir. "I've heard of others too, like Ethereum and Dogecoin".

How Does It Work?

"Cryptos are powered by something called **blockchain**" said Zara. *"It's like a public notebook that records every transaction"*.

"But the notebook is not stored in one place" Rohan explained. "It's copied across thousands of computers around the world".

"No one controls it, and no one can secretly change it" said Ananya. "That's what makes it trustworthy".

"And every transaction is verified by complex calculations" added Aarav. "That's what uses so much electricity".

Why Do People Like Crypto?

Ananya listed some reasons:

- No middlemen like banks

- Fast international transfers
- Some believe it's the future of money
- It can grow quickly in value (and fall just as fast)

"It's like digital gold" said Rohan. "People buy it hoping its value will rise".

"But not everyone uses it to buy things" Zara added. "Most people hold it like an investment".

The Risks

"But crypto is also risky" said Kabir. "It's not backed by any government".

Ananya nodded. "The price can swing wildly. One tweet can make it crash".

"And it's been used in scams too" said Rohan. "Fake coins, hacked wallets, and shady websites".

"That's why many countries are still deciding how to regulate it" Zara said.

What About India?

"In India, crypto is not illegal, but it's also not legal-tender money" explained Ananya.

"The RBI warns people to be careful" said Aarav. "And now, crypto earnings are taxed at 30 percent".

"There's talk of a digital rupee too" Zara said. "But that's different. It will be issued by the RBI, not a private company".

"So India is being cautious but curious" Rohan summed up.

Is Crypto Really Money?

"That depends on what you mean by money" said Ananya.

She wrote:
- **Medium of exchange** – *Kind of, but not widely accepted*
- **Store of value** – *Yes, but risky*
- **Unit of account** – *Not really, because prices are too unstable*

"So it checks some boxes, but not all" Zara said.

"It's more of a digital asset than a full currency" Rohan added.

Quick Recap

Before wrapping up, Ananya summarised:

- Cryptocurrency is digital money built on secure math and code
- It runs on blockchain and doesn't need banks or governments
- It's fast and futuristic, but also volatile and risky
- In India, it's legal to own but not regulated like regular money
- It's more like a digital investment than everyday currency

"Crypto may not be for everyone" said Zara. "But understanding it is important".

"Because it's changing the world of money" said Aarav.

The Piggy Bank Society packed up, still buzzing with questions. They didn't need to become crypto traders. But they were determined to be curious, cautious, and informed.

Chapter 8

Future Wallets – Where Is Money Going Next?

The library felt extra quiet, like it knew this was the final chapter in another Piggy Bank Society journey. The group had learned about ancient coins, digital wallets, and even crypto. Now it was time to look ahead.

"So" Kabir said, looking around, "what comes after QR codes and UPI?"

"Let's talk about the future" said Zara. "Because it's already being built".

Voice, Face, and Fingerprints

Rohan held up his phone. "Some countries are testing voice payments. You say the amount and the person's name, and the money gets sent".

"And in China" Ananya added, "people pay by scanning their face at checkout".

The future of money won't live in wallets. It'll live in your watch, your words, your fingertips and maybe even your smile

"Phones already unlock with fingerprints and face ID" said Aarav. "So why not pay that way too?"

"It's all about making payments more natural and secure" said Zara.

The Digital Rupee

Ananya wrote on the board: **CBDC = Central Bank Digital Currency.**

"It's like cryptocurrency, but controlled by the government" she said. "In India, this is called the **Digital Rupee**".

"It works like cash, but digitally" said Rohan. "You can store it on your phone, even without internet".

"And the best part?" said Aarav. "It's issued by the RBI, so it's fully backed and safe".

"It's still being tested" Zara added. "But it could be the future of everyday money".

Will Physical Money Disappear?

Kabir raised a question. "Will we stop using cash completely?"

"Not so fast" said Ananya. "Many people in India still rely on cash, especially in rural areas".

"But cities might go almost cashless" Rohan said. "And more government services are going digital too".

"So maybe we'll have both" said Aarav. "Cash for some, digital for others".

What About Smart Watches and Wearables?

"Some people already pay with smart watches" said Zara. "You just tap your wrist".

"In the future, maybe you won't even need a device" said Ananya. "Your identity could be your wallet".

"Sounds cool, but also scary" said Kabir.

"That's why privacy and safety will be more important than ever" Rohan said.

Staying Money-Smart in a Fast World

"It's not just about new tools" said Zara. "It's about making sure we stay in control".

Ananya listed a few future-ready money habits:

- Understand how each new tech works before using it
- Don't chase trends blindly
- Keep learning and asking questions
- Never share passwords, pins, or personal data

The Big Picture

Rohan looked thoughtful. "We started with salt and shells. Now we're talking about digital rupees and face scans".

"And through it all" said Zara, "money changed. But what really mattered was trust, awareness, and smart choices".

"We don't know exactly what money will look like ten years from now" Ananya said. "But we know what kind of people we need to be to handle it".

Kabir grinned. "Curious. Cautious. And part of the Piggy Bank Society".

SEASON 2

GOAL BASED SPENDING

Chapter 1

Why Goals Matter

The Piggy Bank Society gathered around the table in their favorite corner of the school library. The walls were lined with colorful posters, but today, the group wasn't focused on any of those. Instead, Ananya had written one big word on the whiteboard: **Goals**.

Kabir looked at it and raised an eyebrow. "So we're going to talk about New Year's resolutions?"

Ananya smiled. "Not exactly, but it's a good start. Today, we're going to talk about why having money goals is so important".

What Are Financial Goals?

Rohan wrote on the board:

Financial Goals = What you want to do with your money.

Goals give your money a purpose. They help you stay focused, make better choices, and celebrate every small step along the way

"It's like setting a target" said Ananya. "When you set a goal, you know exactly what you're saving for. It could be a new bike, a gaming console, or even saving for college in the future".

"I want to save for a trip to the beach this summer" said Kabir.

"Exactly" said Zara. "Your goal is to make that happen. It's all about setting the target, and then figuring out how to get there".

Why Do Goals Matter?

Aarav added, *"Goals are like a roadmap. Without them, you might be driving aimlessly. But with a goal, you know exactly where you want to go"*.

"That's why saving or spending without a plan often leads to mistakes" said Rohan. "When you have a clear goal, it becomes easier to make smart choices".

"Plus" added Zara, "goals give your money meaning. If you're saving for something you really care about, it makes it easier to stick to your plan".

Types of Goals: Short-Term vs. Long-Term

Ananya pointed out, "Not all goals are the same. Some are short-term, and some are long-term".

Short-term goals are those you can achieve in a short amount of time - like saving for a video game, a new book, or a weekend trip.

Long-term goals take more time to achieve - like saving for a car, paying for your college education, or even starting your own business.

"The key is to have both" said Zara. "Short-term goals keep you motivated, while long-term goals help you focus on the big picture".

How Do You Set Goals?

Rohan walked up to the board and drew two columns:

- **Short-Term Goals** (things you can achieve in 1–3 months)
- **Long-Term Goals** (things that will take 1 year or more)

"Now, let's think of some examples" said Ananya. "A short-term goal could be saving ₹500 for a new book. A long-term goal could be saving ₹5,000 for an amusement park next year".

"Short-term goals give you quick wins" added Aarav. "But long-term goals are like planting a seed - they take time to grow".

Setting Goals That Motivate You

Zara said, "The best goals are the ones that excite you. If you're not excited about your goal, it will be hard to keep saving for it".

"Like when I saved up for my guitar" said Kabir. "I could picture myself playing it every day".

"That's what made it worth the effort" said Ananya. "So, it's important to choose goals that mean something to you".

Quick Recap

Rohan summed up:

- Financial goals are what you want to do with your money
- Short-term goals give quick rewards, while long-term goals help you achieve big dreams
- Set goals that excite you and have a plan to get there
- A clear goal makes it easier to stay on track

"Next time" said Ananya, "we'll talk about how to set goals that are clear, achievable, and measurable. Because the clearer your goal is, the easier it is to reach".

The Piggy Bank Society left the library with new energy. For the first time, money wasn't just about spending. It was about achieving something that really mattered.

Chapter 2

How to Set Financial Goals

The next meeting of the Piggy Bank Society started with a challenge. Ananya placed a big glass jar in the middle of the table. Next to it was a stack of colorful paper slips.

"Write down one thing you want to save for and drop it in the jar" she said. One by one, the group wrote and folded their slips.

"A guitar, a smartwatch, a trip to the zoo, a bike, a coding course" read Zara aloud. "These are great goals. But how do we actually get there?"

"Today" said Ananya, "we learn how to set goals the right way".

SMART Goals: The Secret Formula

Rohan wrote the word **SMART** on the whiteboard and broke it down:

Setting a goal means knowing what you want, why you want it, how much it costs, and how long it'll take. That's how dreams turn into plans.

- **S – Specific**: *What exactly are you saving for?*
- **M – Measurable**: *How much money do you need?*
- **A – Achievable**: *Can you actually reach this goal with your income?*
- **R – Relevant**: *Is this goal important to you?*
- **T – Time-bound**: *By when do you want to achieve it*

"If your goal is SMART, it's much easier to work toward" said Zara.

Example Time

Aarav said, "Let's take one from the jar. Say, Kabir's goal is to buy a smartwatch".

Kabir nodded. "It costs around ₹2,000".

"Perfect" said Rohan. "Let's SMART it".

- **Specific**: I want to buy a smartwatch.
- **Measurable**: It costs ₹2,000.
- **Achievable**: I can save ₹200 every week.
- **Relevant**: I'll use it for school and health tracking.
- **Time-bound:** I want to buy it in 10 weeks.

"That's a proper financial plan" said Ananya. "Now you're not just wishing. You're working toward it".

Break Big Goals Into Small Steps

Zara added, "Big goals can feel scary. But if you break them into steps, they feel possible".

Rohan drew a staircase. "Each step is a small milestone. Like saving ₹500, then ₹1,000, then ₹1,500, and finally ₹2,000".

"You feel proud every time you reach a step" said Aarav. "And it keeps you going".

Write It Down

"People who write their goals are more likely to achieve them" said Ananya.

"Use a goal tracker" said Zara. "Draw a bar or fill a jar with coins every time you save a bit".

"Or just use sticky notes on your wall" said Kabir. "Whatever works for you".

Share Your Goal

"Tell someone you trust" said Rohan. "When others know your goal, they can remind you, support you, and celebrate with you".

"Plus, it makes you feel more committed"

said Aarav. "Like making a promise out loud".

Adjust If Needed

"Sometimes things change" said Zara. "If your goal becomes too hard or your income changes, it's okay to adjust the timeline or the target".

"Don't give up. Just rework the plan" said Ananya.

Quick Recap

Rohan wrapped up:

- SMART goals help make your financial dreams real
- Break big goals into small steps
- Track progress in a fun, visual way
- Share your goals for support
- Adjust when needed, but stay focused

"Next session" said Ananya, "we'll talk about needs versus wants. Since knowing the difference helps us decide what's worth saving for".

The Piggy Bank Society scribbled down their SMART goals and pinned them on the wall. With a clear plan, their dreams didn't feel far away anymore. They felt doable.

Chapter 3

The Difference Between Needs and Wants

When the Piggy Bank Society met in the library that afternoon, the table had two big boxes labeled **NEEDS** and **WANTS**.

Next to them was a pile of everyday items written on cards - shoes, chocolates, books, medicines, headphones, birthday gifts.

Ananya smiled as she handed out the cards. "Today, we sort these into the right boxes".

Kabir picked up the first one. "Shoes. That's a need, right?"

"Depends" said Rohan. "Are they your only pair or your fifth fancy one?"

The group laughed and Zara added, "Exactly. Sometimes, it's not about the item. It's about the purpose".

Knowing the difference between what you need and what you simply want is the first step to becoming a smart saver and a smarter spender

What Are Needs?

Aarav wrote on the board:

Needs = Things we must have to live, stay healthy, and go to school or work.

Examples:
- Food and water
- School supplies
- Basic clothing
- Medicine
- Transport to school

"These are non-negotiable" said Zara. "If you don't have them, life becomes hard".

What Are Wants?

Rohan added:

Wants = Things we enjoy, but can live without.

Examples:
- Gaming console
- Designer shoes
- Chocolates every day
- Extra gadgets
- Branded school bag

"Wants make life fun" said Ananya, "but they are not necessary for survival or learning".

"And most of our impulse buys? Total wants" said Kabir.

The Grey Zone

Zara held up a card: **Books**

"Is this a need or a want?" she asked.

"School textbooks? Need. Comic books? Want" said Rohan.

"Exactly. Some things depend on context. That's called the **grey zone**" said Ananya.

Why It Matters

"If we don't know the difference" said Aarav, "we might spend all our money on wants and miss out on needs".

"Or we might save too much and never enjoy the fun stuff" said Kabir.

"It's about balance" said Zara. *"Spend on needs first, save for wants next"*.

The 3-Box Method

Rohan drew three boxes:

- *Must-Have (Needs)*
- *Nice-to-Have (Wants)*
- *Wait-for-It (Dream items)*

"Use this when you're about to buy something" said Ananya. "It helps you pause and think".

Kabir nodded. "Like a filter for your wallet".

Quick Recap

Zara summed it up:

- Needs are essentials like food, school supplies, and health
- Wants are extras that add fun or style
- Some items are in the grey zone and need careful thought
- Spending on needs first helps us stay safe and ready
- Wants can be saved for or enjoyed in balance

The Piggy Bank Society left with a clearer picture of their spending habits. *It wasn't about saying no to fun. It was about knowing when to say yes.*

Chapter 4

The Power of Budgeting

The Piggy Bank Society arrived to find the library transformed into a mini money market. Tables were labeled with signs like "Snacks" "Stationery" "Gadgets" and "Savings Jar".

Each student received a small envelope with fake currency labeled "Pocket Money: ₹500".

"Welcome to Budget Town" said Ananya. "You have ₹500. Let's see how you use it".

What Is a Budget?

Zara wrote on the board:

Budget = A plan for how you will spend and save your money.

"It's like a money map" said Rohan. "It tells your money where to go instead of wondering where it went".

Budgeting is your money roadmap. When every rupee has a job, your goals stay on track and your jars never run dry

"When you don't budget" said Aarav, "you might spend everything before you've paid for what you need".

Budgeting Basics

Ananya introduced the **50-30-20 Rule**:
- *50% for Needs*
- *30% for Wants*
- *20% for Savings*

"Let us say" said Zara, "if you get ₹500:
- ₹250 goes to things you need
- ₹150 can go to things you want
- ₹100 goes straight to savings"

"It's just a guide" added Rohan. "You can adjust it based on your goal or situation".

Try It Yourself

The kids opened their envelopes and walked around Budget Town. Kabir bought stationery and snacks but saved ₹150.

Zara saved first, then spent on a book she really wanted.

Rohan skipped the snacks and added his extra to savings.

"I thought this would be hard" said Kabir. "But it's actually fun".

"That's the point" said Ananya. "Budgeting is like giving yourself permission to spend, just more wisely".

Tracking Your Money

Aarav added, "Once you've made a budget, you have to track what happens".

"Use a notebook, app, or even a daily money log" said Zara. "Write down every rupee you spend or save".

"Knowing where your money goes helps you make better choices next time" said Rohan.

Budgeting for Goals

Kabir asked, "Can we make a budget just for one goal?"

"Absolutely" said Ananya. "If your goal is to save ₹2,000 in two months, your budget might be:

- Earn ₹1,000 per month
- Spend ₹600
- Save ₹400 each month toward the goal"

"That's how your budget helps you reach your dreams" said Zara.

Common Budget Mistakes

Rohan listed a few:
- Not writing things down
- Forgetting about small expenses like snacks
- Spending savings on wants
- Not leaving space for emergencies

"Budgeting takes practice" said Aarav. "The more you do it, the better you get".

Quick Recap

Zara wrapped up:

- Budgeting is a plan for spending and saving your money
- The 50-30-20 rule helps you balance needs, wants, and savings
- Always track your money after you spend it
- Make budgets for specific goals
- Avoid common mistakes and keep improving

The Piggy Bank Society packed up their fake rupees and real lessons. With a budget in hand, their money had a mission.

Chapter 5

Saving for Your Goals

The library buzzed with quiet excitement. Today, Ananya placed a clear piggy bank on the table and dropped a single coin inside. The clink echoed in the room.

"That's the sound of progress" she said. "One rupee at a time".

Kabir smiled. "Saving sounds boring, but that was kind of satisfying".

"Exactly" said Zara. *"Saving is more than keeping money aside. It's how you make your goals come true".*

Why Save?

Rohan wrote on the board:

Saving = Keeping money aside now to use later for something important.

Saving for a goal turns money into motivation. Each coin brings you one step closer to something that truly matters

"When you save, you're buying your future freedom" said Ananya.

"Instead of saying no to something today, you're saying yes to something bigger later" added Zara.

Save First, Spend Later

Aarav shared a tip: *"The best savers save before they spend, not after"*.

Kabir said, "So the moment I get pocket money, I should put some into savings first?"

"Yes" said Rohan. "Even if it's just ₹20 out of ₹100, that habit adds up".

"Make it automatic" added Zara. "Decide your saving percentage and stick to it".

The 80-20 Rule

Ananya introduced a simple formula:
80% for spending, 20% for saving.

"If you get ₹500:
  - ₹400 can be used for needs and wants
  - ₹100 goes directly into your savings jar or account"

"This way, you enjoy the present and build the future" said Aarav.

Label Your Savings

Rohan showed three small jars with labels: "Book Fund" "Guitar" and "Emergency".

"When you label your savings, you stay focused" he said.

"Each jar is a mini-goal" said Zara. "And watching them fill up feels amazing".

"You can even use envelopes, boxes, or digital tools" added Ananya.

Track Your Progress

Kabir asked, "How do I know I'm getting closer to my goal?"

"Create a savings tracker" said Zara. "Draw a bar or use a chart where you color in blocks as you save".

"Small wins feel great" said Aarav. "Every ₹50 closer is something to celebrate".

Avoid Raiding the Jar

Rohan warned, "Don't dip into your goal savings for snacks or sudden wants".

"That's why it helps to have a small 'fun fund' too" said Ananya. "So you don't feel like you're punishing yourself".

"Discipline doesn't mean being boring. It means choosing wisely" said Zara.

Quick Recap

Ananya summarised:
- Saving is the engine of your goals
- Save first, then spend
- Use the 80-20 rule to start simple
- Label and track your savings for motivation
- Stay consistent and protect your savings from impulse temptations

"Next up" said Rohan, "we'll talk about spending - not just how, but how to make choices that don't hurt your goals".

The Piggy Bank Society left the session with a clink in their step. The sound of saving was now music to their ears.

Chapter 6

Smart Spending Choices

The library had a different setup this time. Ananya had arranged a pretend shop with small items labeled with fake prices - snacks, stationery, gadgets, and some shiny trinkets.

"Today" she said, "you can buy whatever you want, but you only have ₹300 in play money. Choose wisely".

Kabir rushed to the gadget section but paused. "Wait, do I need this or just want it because it looks cool?"

"Exactly" said Zara. "Let's talk about smart spending".

What Is Smart Spending?

Rohan wrote on the board:

Smart Spending = Making choices with your money that match your goals and values.

Being smart with spending means thinking beyond the price tag. Good choices help your money go further and feel better too

"It's not about never spending" said Ananya. "It's about spending in a way that helps you - not hurts you later".

"Every rupee is a decision" said Aarav. "Smart spending means making that decision count".

Delay the Decision

Zara shared a tip: *"Before buying something, wait 24 hours if it's not a need".*

"Most of the time, you'll realize you don't need it" said Rohan.

Kabir nodded. "I almost bought glitter pens last week. But I forgot about them the next day".

"That's called **delayed gratification**" said Ananya. "It helps your savings grow too".

Ask the Big Questions

Aarav introduced the checklist:
- *Do I really need this?*
- *Will I still want it in a week?*
- *Is this helping or hurting my goal?*
- *Can I get it for a better price?*
- *What else could I do with this money?*

"Smart spending starts with smart thinking" said Zara.

Plan for Small Joys

"Spending is also about joy" said Rohan.

"And that's okay".

"Just plan for it" said Ananya. "Create a 'fun money' section in your budget".

"If you plan to spend ₹100 on treats, it won't mess up your savings" said Kabir.

"It also helps avoid guilt and sneak spending" said Aarav.

Watch Out for Traps

Zara pointed out common traps:

- Flash sales and limited-time offers
- Buying just because friends are
- Being influenced by packaging or ads
- Thinking expensive means better

"The more you notice the trick, the less power it has" said Ananya.

Celebrate a Good Spend

Kabir said, "I spent ₹150 on a chess set last month. I use it every day".

"That's a great example" said Rohan. "A good spend gives you lasting value".

"When you spend in line with your goals, it feels good" said Zara. "And it makes you want to do it again".

Quick Recap

Ananya summed it up:

- Smart spending is spending that supports your goals
- Delay, question, and plan before buying
- Include fun money in your budget
- Avoid common marketing tricks
- Good spending brings joy and value

"Next up" said Rohan, "we'll look at how investing can help you reach long-term goals faster. Even small amounts can grow big with time".

The Piggy Bank Society packed their pretend purchases and real lessons. Every rupee they spent was starting to feel like a smart choice.

Chapter 7

Investing in Your Future

The library had a quiet buzz as the Piggy Bank Society walked in. On the table were two pots - *one with a seed just planted and another with a small blooming plant.*

"What do you notice?" asked Ananya.

"This one has already grown" said Kabir, pointing at the plant.

"And the other will take time" said Zara. "But it will get there too".

"Just like investing" said Rohan. "Let's dig in".

What Is Investing?

Ananya wrote on the board:

Investing = Putting your money into something that can grow over time.

Investing isn't just about money - it is about growing what matters most with patience, planning, and time

"It could be a business, stocks, mutual funds, or even your own education" said Zara.

"Saving keeps your money safe. Investing helps it grow" added Aarav.

Why Start Early?

Rohan explained, *"The earlier you start investing, the more time your money has to grow"*.

"That's because of something magical called **compound growth**" said Ananya. "It's when your money earns money - and that extra money also earns money".

"Like a snowball rolling downhill" said Kabir. "It gets bigger and faster".

Simple Ways to Start

Zara shared some starter options:

- Piggy bank for a small goal
- Fixed deposits or recurring deposits in a bank
- Mutual funds (with help from parents)
- Learning skills that can earn money

"Investing is not just about money" said Rohan. "Time and learning are investments too".

Risk and Reward

Aarav added, "Some investments are safe, like bank savings. Others have more risk but can give higher rewards".

Ananya explained:

- **Low Risk**: Savings account, FD
- **Medium Risk:** Mutual funds
- **High Risk**: Stocks, new businesses

"You have to know your comfort level" said Zara. "And learn before you leap".

Don't Panic When It Drops

"Sometimes your investment goes down before it goes up" said Rohan.

"That's normal" said Ananya. "Think of it like growing a plant. Some days are dry. Some are rainy. But if you stay consistent, it will grow".

"Don't check it every hour" said Kabir. "It's like weighing yourself after every bite".

Everyone laughed.

Invest in Yourself

"Want to know the best investment ever?" asked Zara. "You".

"Your knowledge, your health, your skills" said Aarav. "All these give returns for life".

"Read. Learn. Try. That's investing too" said Rohan.

Quick Recap

Ananya closed with:

- Investing is how money grows over time
- Start early to get the most out of compound growth
- Choose investments based on your comfort with risk
- Don't panic during ups and downs
- Invest in yourself too - your skills matter

"Next time" said Zara, "we'll talk about how to review and reset your goals. Because every smart money journey needs a checkpoint".

The Piggy Bank Society looked at the tiny seedling again. Just like their future wealth, it had already started growing.

Chapter 8

Reviewing and Reaching Your Goals

The library felt a little more reflective than usual. The Piggy Bank Society sat around the table, sipping lemonade and looking at their savings trackers, notebooks, and colorful goal charts from previous sessions.

"It's been quite a journey" said Ananya. "But today's session might be the most important one yet - **reviewing your goals**".

Kabir looked at his tracker. "I'm almost there with my smartwatch fund".

"And I reached my book savings last week" said Zara proudly.

"Let's talk about what went well, what didn't, and how we can improve" said Rohan.

Reaching a goal is a time to celebrate and to learn. Reflect, adjust, and keep moving forward toward what matters most

Why Review Your Goals?

Aarav wrote on the board:

Reviewing = Checking in on your progress and making changes if needed.

"Without a review, goals can drift. You forget, or life changes" said Ananya.

"Reviewing keeps you on track and helps you adjust instead of giving up" added Zara.

Celebrate the Milestones

Rohan said, "Every step matters. Did you save ₹100? Great. That's progress".

Kabir added, "Even if the final goal is far, small wins keep you motivated".

"Make a celebration chart" suggested Ananya. "Color in a star every time you save or hit a target".

Recheck Your Priorities

"Sometimes" said Zara, "what mattered to you before might not matter as much now".

Aarav nodded. "I was saving for a drone, but now I want to buy drawing equipment instead".

"That's okay" said Rohan. "Goals can evolve. What matters is adjusting your plan".

Restart Without Guilt

"Maybe you stopped saving for a few weeks. That doesn't mean you failed" said Ananya.

"Pick it back up. **Restart**" said Kabir. "It's better than quitting forever".

"Money habits take time" said Zara. "Forgive your mistakes and keep going".

Reset Deadlines If Needed

"Sometimes you need more time" said Rohan. "That's totally fine".

"Stretch your goal from 2 months to 3 months if needed" said Aarav. "Progress over pressure".

Make Goal-Setting a Habit

Ananya encouraged, *"Don't just set goals once. Make it a monthly check-in"*.

"New month, new review" said Zara.

"Ask: **What's working? What's not? What do I want now?"**

"You'll grow with your goals" said Rohan.

Quick Recap

Zara wrapped up:

- Reviewing helps you stay focused and adapt your goals
- Celebrate milestones to stay motivated
- It's okay to change your mind or timeline
- Don't feel guilty about slowdowns - restart and move forward
- Make reviewing a regular habit

Ananya added, "Your goals will change as you grow. That's the beauty of it".

The Piggy Bank Society smiled. They had learned, saved, spent wisely, and invested. But most of all, they had grown. And now, they had the mindset to guide them for the years ahead.

SEASON 3

VALUE OF SAVINGS

Chapter 1

The Secret Superpower of Savings

The Piggy Bank Society had gathered in their usual spot - a cozy corner in the school library. The old wooden table in the center was piled high with books, notebooks, and a half-eaten packet of chips (courtesy of Ananya, who insisted she thought better when munching on something).

"Okay, team" said Rohan, adjusting his glasses. "Today's topic is *Savings*".

"Ugh, sounds boring" groaned Kabir, slumping in his chair. "I mean, why save money when you can just spend it on fun stuff?"

Ananya rolled her eyes. "That's exactly what we need to figure out - why saving is actually important. And why the smartest people in the world swear by it".

Saving money might not look flashy but it quietly builds your power, your choices, and your freedom

The One Marshmallow or Two

Ishaan flipped open his notebook. "Ever heard of the *Marshmallow Test*? It was conducted in the 1970s by a psychologist named *Walter Mischel at Stanford University.* They brought in a group of kids, gave each one a marshmallow, and told them they had two choices : *eat it immediately, or wait 15 minutes and get a second one"*.

"So obviously, they ate it" Kabir said, popping a chip into his mouth.

"Not all of them" Ishaan continued. "Some kids waited. The researchers followed these kids for years, and guess what? The ones who waited had higher *SAT scores, better jobs, and healthier relationships"*.

Ananya smirked. "Basically, they were better at self-control. And guess what? That's the exact skill you need to be good at saving money".

Warren Buffett & Dhirubhai Ambani - Savings Masters

"Wait, wait, wait" Rohan interjected. "So you're telling me that saving money is actually a skill?"

"Exactly!" Ananya nodded. "Look at **Warren Buffett**. He started making money when he was just 6 years old, selling chewing gum door-to-door. By 11, he bought his first stock. But instead of spending all his earnings, he saved and reinvested them. Today, he's one of the richest men in the world".

Kabir whistled. "And what about someone from India?"

"**Dhirubhai Ambani**" Ishaan replied. "He started small, working at a petrol pump in Yemen. But he was smart about money because he saved and reinvested, eventually creating **Reliance Industries,** which is now one of India's biggest companies".

"So you're saying *saving money isn't just for rich people but it's how people become rich?*" Kabir asked.

"Exactly" Rohan said, grinning. "Finally, you're getting it".

The First Ever 'Piggy Bank'

Ananya tapped on her phone. "Did you know the first piggy banks were actually jars made of a type of clay called *'pygg'*?"

"Wait, so the name *piggy bank* comes from a type of clay?" Ishaan asked, surprised.

"Yep! Back in 15th-century England, people didn't have banks like today. Instead, they kept money in 'pygg' clay jars. Over time, someone got creative and shaped them like pigs, and that's how the piggy bank was born".

Kabir raised an eyebrow. "So it has nothing to do with actual pigs?"

"Nope" Ananya said. "But the idea of storing money in a special container has been around for centuries".

Why Our Brain LOVES Spending (And How to Trick It)

"So if saving is so great, why do most of us just spend everything?" Kabir asked.

"Blame your brain" Rohan said, pointing to his head. "When you buy something exciting, your brain releases *dopamine* - the 'feel-good' chemical".

"Which is why shopping feels so awesome" Ananya added. "Dopamine gives you that happy rush, making you want to do it again and again".

"So how do we fight it?" Ishaan asked.

"Simple" Rohan said. ***"Delayed gratification***. If you really want something, wait a week before buying it. Most of the time, you'll realize you don't need it after all".

"And every time you save, you train your brain to enjoy it" Ananya added. "It's like building a muscle".

The Piggy Bank Society Challenge

"So, are we actually gonna start saving, or is this just another talk session?" Kabir asked.

Ishaan smirked. "Let's make it interesting. ***One month savings*** challenge. Every week, save a small amount from your pocket money".

"At the end of the month, we compare" Rohan said. "Winner gets bragging rights".

"And an extra marshmallow" Ananya added, laughing.

"Deal" said Kabir. "Let's do this".

And just like that, The Piggy Bank Society had its first challenge. The mission? Outsmart their spending habits and unlock the ***superpower of savings.***

Chapter 2

The Great Savings Experiment

The Piggy Bank Society was back at their usual spot in the library, notebooks open, calculators out, and minds racing. Their one-month savings challenge had officially begun, and the competition was fierce.

"I hope you all have been sticking to the plan" Ananya said, looking around suspiciously.

Kabir grinned. "Define 'sticking to the plan'".

Rohan groaned. "Kabir, if you've already spent your savings, I swear".

"Relax, relax" Kabir said, waving his hands. "I haven't spent all of it".

Ishaan smirked. "This is exactly why we need to learn how to save properly".

Saving isn't just a habit, it's a skill. And like every good experiment, it gets better with practice

The First Rule of Savings: Pay Yourself First

"Alright, let's start with something simple" Rohan said, pulling out a whiteboard marker. "There's a golden rule when it comes to saving money: *Pay Yourself First*".

Kabir raised an eyebrow. "Wait, aren't I already paying myself when I buy something nice?"

"Nope" Ananya said. "That's called spending. Paying yourself first means the moment you get your pocket money, you set aside a portion for saving before you spend on anything else".

Ishaan chimed in, "Think of it this way - when you eat a meal, you don't leave your own plate empty while serving everyone else first, right? You take your share first".

"That's a good way to put it" Ananya nodded. "Even Warren Buffett follows this rule. He once said, *'Do not save what is left after spending, but spend what is left after saving'"*.

Kabir sighed. "Fine, fine. I'll start setting aside money first".

The 50-30-20 Rule: A Simple Savings Formula

"So how much should we save?" Rohan asked, flipping to a new page in his notebook. "10%? 50%? All of it?"

"Well, there's something called the *50-30-20 Rule*" Ishaan explained. "It's a super easy way to manage money".

"Let me guess, it involves percentages?" Kabir groaned.

"Exactly" Ananya said. "Here's how it works:
- **50% for Needs**: Stuff you *have* to buy, like food, transport, school supplies.
- **30% for Wants**: Fun things, like snacks, games, or a movie.
- **20% for Savings**: This goes straight to your savings".

Kabir looked thoughtful. "Wait, so if I get ₹500 as pocket money, I should save ₹100?"

"Bingo!" Rohan said. "And imagine doing that every month for a whole year. That's ₹1,200 saved without even thinking about it".

Compound Interest: The Magic of Making Money Grow

"But here's where it gets cool" Ananya continued. "Ever heard of *Compound Interest*?"

Kabir shook his head. "Sounds like a science experiment".

"In a way, it is" Ishaan said. "Imagine you put ₹100 in a savings account. Let's say it earns 10% interest per year. After the first year, you get ₹10 extra, so you have ₹110".

"Okay, simple enough" Kabir said.

"But in the second year, you don't just earn interest on the ₹100. You earn it on ₹110. So now you get ₹11 instead of ₹10".

Kabir's eyes widened. "Wait… so every year, the interest grows bigger?"

"Exactly!" Rohan grinned. "That's the power of **compounding**. The earlier you start saving, the more money you'll have in the future".

"It is believed that even Albert Einstein called it the *Eighth Wonder of the World*" Ananya added. "He said, *'He who understands it, earns it. He who doesn't, pays it.'*"

Kabir sat back in his chair. "Okay, now this is actually interesting".

The Latte Factor: Tiny Expenses, Big Losses

"But if we're saving money, we also have to stop wasting it" Ishaan said. "Ever heard of the *Latte Factor*?"

Kabir frowned. "Something to do with coffee?"

"Sort of" Ananya said. "It's a term by *David Bach*, and it means that small, unnecessary expenses can add up to huge amounts over time. Like, if you spend ₹50 every day on snacks, that's ₹1,500 a month and ₹18,000 a year".

Kabir's jaw dropped. "₹18,000 just on snacks?!"

"Exactly. Imagine if you saved half of that instead" Rohan said.

Kabir groaned. "Fine, maybe I'll cut back a little".

The Piggy Bank Society's Savings Plan

"So here's the plan" Rohan said, writing on the board. "For the next month, we follow three rules:

- **Pay Yourself First** – Save at least 20% of any money we get.
- **Track Our Spending** – No unnecessary purchases without thinking twice.
- **Try Compounding** – Put our savings in a place where it can grow".

Ishaan grinned. "And whoever saves the most gets a surprise reward".

"What's the reward?" Kabir asked, suspiciously.

Ananya smirked. "Let's just say, you'll want to save for it".

The challenge was on. The Piggy Bank Society wasn't just talking about saving anymore - they were *doing* it. And little did they know, they were about to discover just how powerful savings could be!

Chapter 3

Smart Spending - The Art of Making Every Rupee Count

The Piggy Bank Society was back in their cozy hideout - a quiet corner of the school library where ideas bounced off the walls like an intense game of badminton. Today's topic? *Spending wisely.*

"Why do we spend money the way we do?"

Aarav leaned back in his chair, tossing a rubber band between his fingers. "So, last time we talked about savings. But what about spending? I mean, we all need to spend, right?"

"Of course!" said Ananya, flipping through a book on behavioral economics. "But the real question is, do we spend *wisely*?"

Kabir, the history buff of the group, jumped in. "You know, there's an old saying - *A fool and his money are soon parted.* People have been talking about smart spending for centuries!"

Spending smart isn't about saying no to everything, it's about saying yes to the things that matter most

Impulse Buying & The Psychology of Spending

"Okay, let's talk impulse buying" Zara said, pulling out a chocolate bar from her bag. "You ever go to a store, see something shiny near the counter, and just have to buy it?"

"Every single time!" Aarav admitted.

"That's called *impulse buying* - when you buy something without planning.

And guess what? It's not your fault entirely. Shops design their layouts to make you spend more!"

Ananya nodded. "Yep. It's all about psychology. They use bright colors, big discounts, and even smells to make us feel like we need something we actually don't. Ever notice how bakeries smell amazing? That's intentional!"

"So how do we fight back?" Kabir asked.

"Try the 10-second rule" Zara suggested. "Before buying anything non-essential, take 10 seconds to ask yourself - Do I really need this? Will I regret this later? If the answer is maybe or no, walk away!"

Warren Buffett's Secret to Spending

Aarav pulled out his phone. "I read that Warren Buffett still lives in the same house he bought in 1958.

The guy's a billionaire but doesn't waste money. Instead, he focuses on value".

"Exactly!" Ananya said. "He once said, *If you buy things you do not need, soon you will have to sell things you need.* Smart spending isn't about being cheap - it's about buying what truly matters".

Needs vs. Wants

Kabir grabbed a whiteboard marker. "Let's make a list. Needs vs. Wants".

- **Needs**: Food, shelter, education, healthcare.
- **Wants**: Fancy sneakers, latest phone, premium subscriptions.

"See the difference? We should *prioritise needs over wants*. But that doesn't mean never buying fun stuff - it means planning for it".

The Envelope System – A Spending Hack

Zara's eyes lit up. "My grandma used an *envelope system*. She'd keep cash in different envelopes - one for groceries, one for travel, one for savings. Once an envelope was empty, no more spending".

"That's genius!" Kabir said. "And we can do the same digitally. Just create different bank accounts or use apps to track expenses".

Wrapping Up: The Smart Spender's Golden Rule

Aarav stood up dramatically. "So, today's golden rule is: *Spend less than you earn and always check if your spending adds value to your life*. And remember the 10-second rule before impulse buying!".

Chapter 4

The Magic of Investing - Making Your Money Work for You

The Piggy Bank Society was back in their favorite corner of the library, notebooks open and minds buzzing. Today's mission? Understanding *investing* - a topic that sounded intimidating but had the power to change lives.

Kabir tapped his pen against the table. "So, we've talked about saving and smart spending. But my uncle says **saving alone won't make you rich**. He keeps talking about something called investing".

"He's right!" Zara said. "Think of your money as a seed. If you just store it in a drawer, it stays the same. But if you plant it, water it, and let it grow, it can turn into a huge tree! That's what investing does - it makes your money grow".

Investing isn't instant. But with planning, patience, and discipline, even small amounts can grow into something big

The Story of Warren Buffett – The World's Greatest Investor

Aarav leaned in. "You guys know Warren Buffett right? The guy started investing when he was 11 years old. And now he's worth over $100 billion!"

"What?!" Ananya's eyes widened. "He was practically the same age as us when he started"

"Buffett bought his first stock for $38 and held onto it. He didn't try to make quick money - he played the long game. That's the secret to investing: *Patience + Time*".

The Power of Compounding – The 8th Wonder of the World

Kabir pulled up a calculator app. "Okay, let's say I invest ₹1,000 today, and I get a 10% return every year. How much will I have in 20 years?"

Aarav punched in the numbers. "Hold on… ₹6,727!"

"That's the power of **compounding** - you earn interest not just on your original ₹1,000 but also on the interest you earn each year. No wonder it is called as the 8th wonder of the world".

Stocks vs. Bonds vs. Mutual Funds – What's What?

"Okay, but where do you even invest?" Zara asked.

Ananya broke it down:

- **Stocks** – Buying a tiny piece of a company. High risk, high reward.
- **Bonds** – Lending money to companies/government. Low risk, low reward.
- **Mutual Funds** – A mix of stocks and bonds managed by experts. Good for beginners.

"So stocks are like roller coasters - exciting but risky" Aarav said. "Bonds are like a slow train - steady and safe. And mutual funds are like a guided tour - you let an expert handle the ride".

Risk vs. Reward – Don't Put All Your Eggs in One Basket

Kabir frowned. "But what if I invest in a stock and lose all my money?"

"That's why you **diversify**" Zara explained. "It means spreading your money across different investments. If one fails, the others can still make up for it. *Never put all your eggs in one basket!*"

The Rule of 72 – Doubling Your Money

Ananya grinned. "Wanna know a cool trick? It's called the **Rule of 72**. Divide 72 by your investment's interest rate, and that's how many years it takes to double your money!"

"So if I get 8% returns, 72 ÷ 8 = 9 years" Aarav calculated. "That means my money doubles in 9 years! That's insane!"

Conclusion: Becoming an Investor Starts Now

Zara stood up dramatically. "Moral of the story? *Don't just save money. Make your money work for you!*"

Aarav grinned. "Time to start our first investments?"

Kabir laughed. "Only if you promise not to spend it all on video games!"

As they packed up their notebooks, the Piggy Bank Society knew they had uncovered a secret weapon - *investing*. And this was just the beginning of their financial adventure!

Chapter 5

The Money Mindset - How Your Brain Affects Your Wallet

The Piggy Bank Society gathered in their usual spot, buzzing with excitement. Today's discussion wasn't about numbers or accounts - it was about something even more powerful: the ***psychology of money***.

"Money isn't just math - it's mindset"

Zara tapped the whiteboard. "Guys, have you ever wondered why some people save every rupee while others spend like there's no tomorrow? It's not just about how much money they have - it's about how they think about money".

"So you're saying money decisions aren't just about logic?" Aarav raised an eyebrow.

"Exactly! It's like food. You know eating too much junk is bad, but you still crave it, right? Money works the same way. Your brain plays tricks on you".

Our thoughts shape our habits. And our habits decide whether we build wealth or just chase wants

The Scarcity Mindset vs. The Abundance Mindset

"Okay, here's something crazy" Kabir said. "People who believe money is scarce always feel like they don't have enough - even when they do. They hold on too tight, scared to invest or take risks".

"And then there's the *abundance mindset*" Ananya added. "These people believe there's always more money to be made, so they invest, learn, and grow their wealth".

"So which mindset do we need?" Aarav asked.

"Abundance!" Zara said. "Think about it - if you believe there are always new opportunities, you'll take action instead of being scared".

Why People Make Dumb Money Decisions

"Here's a fun fact" Ananya grinned. "Your brain releases *dopamine* when you buy something you really want. It's the same chemical that makes you feel happy when you eat chocolate or get a like on Instagram".

"Wait, so shopping literally makes us feel happiness?" Kabir laughed.

"Exactly! That's why some people shop when they're sad - it's called *emotional spending*. But the happiness doesn't last, and then they regret it".

"So the trick is to recognize when we're being emotional?" Aarav asked.

"Yes! Before buying something, ask yourself: 'Do I need this, or do I just feel like I need it?'"

Money and Happiness – What's the Link?

"Speaking of emotions" Kabir said, "does money really make people happy?"

"Up to a point, yes" Zara said. "Studies show that people are happier when they *earn enough to meet their needs comfortably*. But after that, more money doesn't always mean more happiness".

"That's because experiences bring more happiness than things" Aarav added. "Spending on travel, learning, or helping others feels better than buying stuff".

Conclusion: Master Your Money Mindset

Zara stood up. "So, what did we learn today? Money isn't just about what's in your wallet - it's about what's in your head!"

Kabir nodded. "If we understand our brain's tricks, we can **control our spending, save wisely, and invest smartly**".

"And that's how we build real wealth!" Ananya grinned.

As they packed up, the Piggy Bank Society knew that money wasn't just numbers - it was psychology, mindset, and smart decisions. And they were ready to use this knowledge to their advantage.

Chapter 6

The Ultimate Superpower - Discipline with Money

The Piggy Bank Society had gathered one last time for this book. Tonight, they weren't just talking about saving or spending wisely. They were talking about something bigger.

"Okay, gang" Zara said, leaning forward. "We've cracked how to save money and control our spending. But what if I told you there's a way to make our money grow while we sleep?"

Kabir's eyes lit up. "You mean investing, right?"

"Exactly!" Zara said. "Most people work hard for money, but *smart people make their money work for them*. That's the real game".

The ultimate money power isn't just in how much you have - it's in knowing how to save, grow, and repeat

Lesson 1: The Magic of Compound Interest

"Let's start with a question" Zara continued. "Would you rather have ₹1 crore today or ₹1 that doubles every day for a month?"

"Easy! ₹1 crore" Aarav said.

Zara smirked. "Wrong. If you choose ₹1 that doubles daily, by Day 30, you'll have... *₹53 crores*! That's compound interest".

Kabir's jaw dropped. "Wait, what?! That's insane!"

Ananya grabbed a notebook. "So if we invest early, our money has more time to grow, right?"

"Bingo!" Zara nodded. "Even small amounts invested early become huge over time. That's why Warren Buffett, started investing when he was just 11 years old".

Lesson 2: Risk and Reward – The Balancing Act

"Okay, but isn't investing risky?" Kabir asked. "What if we lose money?"

"Great question!" Zara said. "**Risk and reward always go together.** Low risk means low returns. High risk can mean big rewards - but also bigger losses. The trick is to find a balance based on your goals".

"And also not to panic" Ananya added. "Like, if the market goes down today, it doesn't mean we sell everything, right?"

"Exactly!" Zara said. "Investing is a long game. Warren Buffett says, *'The stock market is a device for transferring money from the impatient to the patient.'*"

Lesson 3: The Importance of Financial Freedom

"Okay, final question" Zara said. "Why do we save and invest in the first place? What's the big goal?"

"To be rich?" Aarav guessed.

"Not exactly" Zara smiled. "It's about *financial freedom.* That means having enough money to live life on your own terms. No worrying about bills, no need to do a job you hate. It's the ability to choose".

"Like being able to take a year off to travel, or start a business, or retire early?" Ananya asked.

"Yes!" Zara nodded. "Money itself isn't the goal. Freedom is".

The Final Takeaway: Be the Boss of Your Money

As the discussion wrapped up, the Piggy Bank Society realized they weren't just talking about rupees and paise anymore. They were talking about how to live **smarter, happier lives.**

"So what's the biggest lesson from everything we learned?" Zara asked.

Kabir grinned. "Simple: *Money isn't just something you earn and spend. It's a tool. Learn how to use it, and you can shape your own future*".

"And the earlier we start, the better" Ananya added. "Because time is the most powerful weapon we have".

"And that's why we're called the Piggy Bank Society" Aarav said. "We're not just saving money. We're saving **knowledge about money**".

Zara smiled. "And now, it's time to use that knowledge".

SCIENCE OF BORROWING

Chapter 1

Wait, You Can Borrow Money?

The Piggy Bank Society was back in session. The same library corner, the same long wooden table, the same rattly fan spinning above them. But today, the air felt a bit different, like they were about to uncover something big.

"So" Aarav began, stretching out in his chair, "I overheard my uncle talking about taking a loan for a new car. He said the bank would lend him the money and he'd pay it back slowly. That sounds... kind of wild?"

"You're telling me banks just give you money?" Kabir asked. "Like, here you go, buy yourself something nice?"

Zara laughed. "Not exactly. You borrow the money. Then you pay it back. With **interest**."

"What's interest?" Kabir frowned. "Like when I'm interested in chips?"

Borrowing money seems magical at first but every loan comes with responsibility. Borrow now, pay later... sometimes with a little extra

Rohan rolled his eyes. "No, *interest as in extra money you pay because someone let you borrow theirs. Think of it as the price of borrowing.*"

Ananya was already scribbling something on her notebook. "Today's topic," she said, holding up the page: 'T**he Borrowing Game: Why People Take Loans and What It Really Means**'

Why Do People Borrow?

The group took turns listing out reasons.

"House loans" said Zara. "Because no one keeps fifty lakh rupees lying around".

"Education" added Rohan. "College is expensive".

"Emergencies" said Ananya. "Like a medical bill".

"Business" Aarav nodded. "My cousin took a loan to start a bakery".

Kabir looked thoughtful. "So borrowing helps people do things now, even if they don't have the money upfront".

"Exactly" Ananya said. "It's a tool. If used wisely, it can change lives".

Borrowing From Friends vs. Borrowing From Banks

"Okay, but what's the difference between borrowing ₹100 from Kabir" Zara said, "and ₹1,00,000 from a bank?"

"With Kabir, you might get a glare if you don't return it" Rohan smirked.

Everyone laughed.

"But with banks" Ananya continued, "it's formal. There's a contract, rules, penalties, interest, all of it. You don't just promise, you sign".

"Banks also check if you're eligible" said Zara. "Do you have income? Can you repay? What's your credit score?"

"Wait, we're getting scored for borrowing now?" Kabir asked.

"Yup" Rohan nodded. "We'll come to that later".

Borrowing Isn't Bad (But It's Not Free Either)

"Here's the thing" Ananya said. "A lot of people think loans are bad. But they're just tools".

"Like fire" said Zara. "You can cook food or burn the kitchen".

"It depends how you use it" Rohan added. "If you're borrowing to buy a bike you don't need, that's trouble. But for college or a medical bill? That's smart".

"And remember," Aarav added, "loans aren't free. You always pay extra through interest".

A Quick Simulation

"Let's say you borrow ₹10,000 to buy a new laptop" said Ananya. "The bank charges 10 percent annual interest. After a year, you owe ₹11,000".

"₹1,000 extra?" Kabir's eyes widened.

"Yup" Zara nodded. "And if you repay slowly over two years, you might end up paying even more. That's the **cost of convenience**".

"So borrowing helps, but it comes with a price tag" Rohan said.

Quick Recap

Before packing up, Zara summarized:

- Borrowing is taking money now and promising to pay later
- People borrow for homes, education, emergencies, businesses
- Bank borrowing is formal, with interest and rules
- Borrowing can be helpful, but it's never free

Ananya closed her notebook. "Next time, let's go deeper. What's interest? What are EMIs? And how much more are we really paying?"

The Piggy Bank Society nodded, their curiosity lit up like a spark.

This wasn't just about money. It was about understanding choices.

Chapter 2

Price You Pay – Interest, EMIs & the Loan Triangle

The next session of the Piggy Bank Society started with Rohan drawing three arrows on the whiteboard. He labeled them: **Principal, Interest, and Tenure.**

"What's this?" Kabir asked, munching on a biscuit.

"This" Rohan replied, "is the **triangle of borrowing**. You borrow money, pay it back over time, and pay extra for the privilege. That extra is called **interest**".

"Okay, but what exactly is interest?" Aarav asked.

Ananya smiled. "Let's break it down."

Loans aren't just about borrowing - they're about understanding what you'll really pay over time. Know the triangle before you sign

Understanding Interest – The Cost of Borrowing

"Say you borrow ₹10,000 from a bank" Ananya explained. "They'll ask you to return more than that. Maybe ₹11,000 after a year. That ₹1,000 is interest".

"Basically, *it's the rent you pay for using someone else's money*" Zara said.

"It can be calculated in different ways" added Rohan. "The simplest is called **simple interest**. But most banks use **compound interest**".

Kabir frowned. "Why does that sound like maths class?"

"Because it is" Aarav said, grinning. "But this time, it matters in real life".

EMIs – Equated Monthly Installments

"So how do people repay loans?" Kabir asked.

"Usually in small chunks every month" Zara said. "That's called an EMI".

"**Equated Monthly Instalment**" Ananya added. "It includes part of the principal and part of the interest".

She wrote on the board: *EMI = Principal + Interest divided into equal monthly payments*

"For example" Rohan said, "If you take a ₹1,00,000 loan at 10 percent interest for one year, you'll pay around ₹8,800 every month".

"By the end of the year, you would have paid about ₹1,05,600" Zara said. "So the bank earns ₹5,600 on your loan".

"Wow. So the longer I take to pay, the more I end up paying" Kabir said.

"Exactly" Aarav nodded. "And that's where the triangle comes in".

The Loan Triangle – Principal, Interest, and Tenure

"Think of a triangle with three sides" Rohan said. "If you stretch one, the others shift too".

- *Principal is the amount you borrow*
- *Interest Rate is the percentage the bank charges you*
- *Tenure is the time you take to repay*

"If you borrow more, or for longer, or at a higher rate, your EMIs go up" Zara explained.

"And if you want lower EMIs, you may pay more overall because the tenure is longer" said Ananya.

Kabir scribbled a triangle and labeled the corners. "Okay, I get it now. You can't change one side without affecting the others".

A Real-Life Example

"Let's do a quick simulation" Aarav said. "You want to buy a bicycle worth ₹12,000. You don't have the money, so you take a loan for one year at 10 percent".

- Principal = ₹12,000
- Interest = ₹1,200
- Total to repay = ₹13,200
- EMI = ₹1,100 per month

"If you pay it off in 6 months instead, your EMI goes up but your total interest comes down" Zara added.

"So time is money, literally" said Kabir.

"Exactly" Ananya nodded.

Quick Recap

Before they wrapped up, Zara listed what they had learned:

- Interest is the cost of borrowing money
- EMIs break repayment into monthly amounts
- Loan Triangle connects principal, interest rate, and tenure
- Longer loans mean smaller EMIs but more interest overall

"Borrowing is not just about getting money" Ananya said. "It's about understanding what you'll pay back, how, and for how long".

"And that," Rohan added, "is how banks turn lending into a business".

The Piggy Bank Society packed up, already wondering about their next big topic. Kabir had a feeling credit cards were coming next.

Chapter 3

Credit Cards – Swipe Now, Pay Forever?

The Piggy Bank Society gathered for their next session with a lot more curiosity than usual. Kabir had walked in holding a shiny piece of plastic.

"Behold!" he said, holding it up like a trophy. "My cousin's credit card. He just bought a gaming console with it. Said he'll pay it off later. No big deal".

"Big deal indeed" said Ananya. "That tiny card can do big things. Some good, some not so good".

"So today," Zara said, "we talk about one of the most loved and feared tools in modern finance. The credit card".

What Is a Credit Card?

"A **credit card lets you borrow money from the bank**" Rohan explained. "Every time you swipe it, you are basically saying, I'll pay for this later".

Credit cards let you swipe now and pay later but the longer you wait, the more it costs

"You don't spend your own money right away" said Zara. "The bank pays the shop. Then you pay the bank back".

"And if you don't pay on time?" Kabir asked.

"They charge interest. High interest" Ananya said. "**As much as 30 to 40 percent per year**".

"Wait, that's way more than a normal loan" Aarav said.

"Exactly" said Rohan. "Which is why people get into trouble with it".

The Minimum Due Trap

Kabir looked confused. "But there's this thing called **minimum due**, right? My cousin only paid ₹500 on a ₹5,000 bill".

"That's the trap" said Zara. "*If you only pay the minimum, the rest of the amount collects interest. And fast*".

"It feels like you're handling it, but the actual bill keeps growing" added Ananya.

Rohan drew on the board:
- Total bill: ₹5,000
- Minimum due: ₹500
- Balance carried: ₹4,500
- Interest added: ₹150 (just for one month)

"In a few months, you might end up paying ₹6,000 or more" he said. "Just because you didn't pay in full".

Why Credit Cards Feel Easy

"It doesn't feel like real money" Aarav said. "Just a swipe and done".

"That's the psychology" said Ananya. **"You don't see the money leave your wallet. So you spend more than you usually would".**

"And credit cards often come with offers, cashback, reward points" Zara added. "All designed to make you swipe more".

"But if you don't track it, you lose control" Rohan said. "Fast"

When Can Credit Cards Be Useful?

"Okay, so are credit cards always bad?" Kabir asked.

"Not at all" said Zara. "They can be useful if you use them smartly".

Ananya listed a few good uses:

- For emergencies when you don't have cash
- To build a good credit score by repaying on time
- To earn rewards if you pay the full amount every month

"So the key is to treat it like a debit card" said Rohan. **"Only spend what you can repay in full"**.

Quick Recap

Before wrapping up, Ananya summarized:

- Credit cards let you borrow money from the bank
- If not repaid in full, you pay high interest
- Paying only the minimum traps you in debt
- They are useful for emergencies or building credit
- Use them like debit cards and always pay on time

"Credit cards are like matches" said Rohan. "Light a candle or burn your fingers".

The Piggy Bank Society nodded. They were learning that money tools are powerful, but only in the right hands.

Chapter 4

Good Loans vs. Bad Loans

This week, Kabir showed up early and was unusually quiet. He placed a small notebook on the table, tapped it, and said, "My brother took a loan last year to buy a new phone. Now he's still paying EMIs and the phone isn't even that special anymore".

"Classic case," said Zara. "Borrowing for something that loses value fast".

"So today," Ananya said, "we figure out the *difference between borrowing that builds your life and borrowing that breaks it*".

What Makes a Loan Good?

"A good loan helps you grow" said Rohan. "It helps you earn more, learn more, or create something meaningful".

"Education loan? Good" said Ananya. "Home loan? Usually good, because property increases in value over time".

Not all loans are equal. Good loans help you build a better future, while bad loans only feel good for a moment

"Business loan for a well-researched idea? Also good" added Zara. "Because it's an investment in your future".

"And what's common between them?" Aarav asked.

"They lead to growth" Rohan said. "Not just spending".

What Makes a Loan Bad?

"Bad loans are for stuff that doesn't last or doesn't help you grow" Zara explained.

Kabir listed a few:

- Buying the newest phone just for style
- Taking a vacation you can't afford
- Shopping online during sales using credit card EMI

"Basically, borrowing for things that lose value fast or give short-term joy" said Ananya.

"And sometimes, people borrow just to impress others" Aarav added. "That's not smart either".

The 'Borrowing Test'

Ananya wrote five questions on the whiteboard:

- *Will this help me grow or earn in the future?*
- *Will this thing still matter a year from now?*
- *Can I repay this comfortably every month?*
- *Is there a cheaper way to get it?*
- *Am I borrowing out of pressure or emotion?*

"If your answer is mostly 'yes' to the first three, you're probably taking a good loan" said Zara. "If it's more 'yes' to the last two, maybe rethink it".

The EMI Illusion

"I saw a smartwatch for ₹3,000 online" Kabir said. "But it said only ₹270 per month. That felt like nothing".

"That's the trick" Rohan said. "They break it into small EMIs to make it look easy. But you're still paying the full amount. *Sometimes even more, because of hidden fees or processing charges*".

"It's like a sugar-coated trap" Aarav said.

"Exactly" said Ananya. "*Convenient borrowing isn't always smart borrowing*".

Case Studies: Riya and Rahul

"Riya takes a loan to attend a coding bootcamp" Zara narrated. "It costs ₹40,000, but it helps her land a part-time freelance job within six months".

"Rahul borrows ₹25,000 to buy limited-edition sneakers" said Rohan. "He wears them twice and then realizes he can't afford the EMI anymore".

"Who made the smarter borrowing decision?" asked Ananya.

Everyone answered together, "Riya."

"She borrowed to grow. Rahul borrowed to show" Kabir said, proud of his rhyme.

Quick Recap

Before they wrapped up, Ananya summarized:

- Good loans build your future
- Bad loans burn your savings and peace of mind
- Use the borrowing test before making a decision
- Don't get lured by tiny EMIs
- Always ask: *is this helping me or just tempting me?*

"Money is a tool" Zara said. "And borrowing is like using power tools. Helpful when used right. Risky when misused".

The Piggy Bank Society packed up their notes, already seeing their world differently. From flashy gadgets to life goals, they now had a clearer sense of what borrowing was really for.

Next week's topic? Something mysterious but powerful: the credit score.

Chapter 5

The Credit Score Mystery

The next meeting started with Kabir holding a big poster with the number "823" written in red marker.

"Is this good?" he asked.

"That depends" said Rohan. "Are you talking about exam marks or your credit score?"

"Credit score" Kabir replied. "My cousin said his score is 823, and he got a car loan super easily".

"Then yes" Ananya said. "That's very good".

"So what even is a credit score?" Aarav asked.

"Let's find out," said Zara. "Today, we're solving the mystery of the credit score".

Your credit score is like a report card for how responsibly you borrow. Pay on time, and your score becomes your strongest reference

What Is a Credit Score?

"A credit score is a number that shows how trustworthy you are with borrowed money" Rohan explained. *"It usually ranges from 300 to 900"*

"The higher, the better" said Ananya. *"Above 750 is considered excellent"*.

"It's like your financial reputation" Zara added. "Lenders look at it before giving you a loan or a credit card".

"So it's like a report card for borrowing?" asked Kabir.

"Exactly," Aarav replied. "And just like in school, good habits give you good scores".

What Affects Your Credit Score?

Ananya listed the main factors on the whiteboard:

- **Payment History** – Do you pay your EMIs or credit card bills on time?
- **Credit Utilisation** – Are you using too much of your credit limit?
- **Length of Credit History** – How long have you had a credit account?
- **Credit Mix** – Do you have both credit cards and loans?

- **New Credit Inquiries** – Are you applying for too many loans or cards at once?

"So if I use a credit card and repay on time, my score goes up?" Kabir asked.

"Correct" said Zara. "But if you miss payments or max out your credit card, your score drops".

Why Does It Matter?

"A good credit score helps you get loans more easily" said Ananya. "And at lower interest rates".

"It's not just about getting the loan" Rohan added. "It's about saving money in the long run".

"Even landlords and some employers check credit scores" said Zara. "It shows if you're responsible".

"So it's kind of a life skill" Aarav said. "Build a good score and life gets a bit smoother".

How Do You Check Your Score?

"In India, credit scores are provided by agencies like **CIBIL, Experian, and CRIF**" said Ananya. *"You can check your score online for free once a year"*.

"You'll need your PAN card and basic details" added Zara. "No need to pay unless you want a detailed report".

"And checking your own score doesn't lower it" Rohan said. "That's a myth".

Piggy Bank Society's Credit Score Game

"Let's play a quick game" said Aarav. "Imagine you are grown up and using credit".

Each person picked a card from a deck Ananya had made.
- *Zara's card*: Pays EMIs on time for 2 years – Score: 780
- *Rohan's card*: Misses one credit card payment – Score: 690
- *Kabir's card*: Applies for 5 new loans in a month – Score: 650
- *Ananya's card*: Maintains low usage and has an old credit card – Score: 810

"Small actions make a big difference" Ananya said.

"And the key is consistency" Zara added. "One good month won't fix everything".

Quick Recap

Before closing, Rohan summarized:

- A credit score shows your trustworthiness with money
- Scores range from 300 to 900; aim for above 750
- Timely payments and low credit usage help
- Missing payments, applying too often, or maxing out cards hurt your score
- A good score means lower interest and better opportunities

"Credit is power" said Ananya. "And your score is how well you handle that power".

"Like a superhero rating" Kabir said. "I want to be in the 800 club".

The Piggy Bank Society laughed, their minds buzzing with numbers and new possibilities.

Next up: borrowing in the real world, and how it works across India.

Chapter 6

Borrowing in India – Who Gets Loans and Why

The next session began with Ananya walking in with a stack of newspapers and printouts. She dropped them on the table and said, "We've been talking about borrowing like it's the same for everyone. But in India, it's very different depending on who you are and where you live"

"Different how?" asked Kabir.

"Let's find out," said Zara. "Because borrowing isn't just a personal thing. It's also social, economic, and sometimes even political".

Who Borrows Money in India?

Rohan pulled up a chart on his tablet. "People across India borrow for different reasons"
- **In urban areas:** house loans, car loans, education loans, credit cards
- **In rural areas:** farming inputs, emergencies, weddings, festivals

In India, access to loans depends on who you are, what you do, and how systems are built. Understanding this helps us build a fairer future

"In cities, people borrow to grow" said Ananya. "In villages, people often borrow to survive".

"And that's why their access to loans matters so much" added Zara.

Formal vs. Informal Lending

"In cities, people usually borrow from banks and NBFCs" said Aarav. "These are formal lenders with rules and paperwork".

"In rural areas, many still borrow from local moneylenders" Ananya explained. "They give fast cash but charge very high interest".

"How high?" Kabir asked.

"Sometimes over 100 percent a year" Zara said. "And if you can't repay, they can get aggressive".

"That's scary" Rohan said.

"It's called the **debt trap**" Ananya said. "People borrow more just to repay old loans. It never ends".

What Is Microfinance?

"Microfinance is a game changer" said Zara. "*It gives small loans to people who don't qualify for bank loans*".

"Like a tailor needing a sewing machine" said Rohan. "Or a small kirana store owner who needs to restock".

"These loans are usually between ₹10,000 and ₹50,000" said Ananya. "And they're repaid in weekly or monthly instalments".

"Institutions like SKS Microfinance and Grameen Bank do this" added Aarav. "They help people become self-reliant".

Government Schemes That Help

Ananya handed out a sheet with three popular government loan programs:

1. *Pradhan Mantri Mudra Yojana* – For small businesses
2. *Kisan Credit Card* – For farmers
3. *Education Loan Subsidy Schemes* – For students from low-income families

"These programs reduce interest or help with repayment" Zara explained. "But not everyone knows they exist".

"So awareness is as important as access" Rohan said.

Challenges in Getting a Loan

Kabir asked, "Why can't everyone just walk into a bank and get a loan?"

Ananya listed the barriers:
- No credit history
- No steady income or job
- No collateral like property or gold
- No identity or address proof

"And sometimes, the bank is just too far away" said Aarav. "That's why digital lending is slowly helping".

Stories from the Ground

Zara shared a real story. "In Maharashtra, a group of women formed a self-help group. They took a joint loan to start a papad business. Now, they earn enough to send their kids to school".

"That's amazing," said Kabir. "So borrowing can be empowering".

"Yes," said Ananya. "When it's fair, affordable, and well-used".

"But when it's not," Rohan added, "it can destroy families".

Quick Recap

Zara closed the session with a summary:

- Borrowing needs are different in urban and rural India
- Many still rely on informal moneylenders with high risks
- Microfinance and government schemes support those without access
- Barriers like documents, credit scores, and awareness block many
- Fair borrowing can lift people up, while unfair borrowing can trap them

"Borrowing is more than a bank transaction" said Ananya. *"It's a window into someone's life situation"*.

"And when we understand that," Rohan added, "we become not just money smart, but socially aware too".

The Piggy Bank Society sat quietly for a moment, thinking. Finance wasn't just about numbers anymore. It was about people.

Chapter 7

Borrowing Smart –
A Practical Guide

It was Zara's turn to lead the session, and she began by placing two envelopes on the table.

"One of these," she said, "is a smart loan. The other is a mistake waiting to happen. Let's find out how to tell the difference".

Kabir opened the first envelope. Inside was a note: "Loan of ₹50,000 to buy a second-hand food truck and start a weekend sandwich stall".

Rohan opened the second: "Loan of ₹1,20,000 to buy the latest phone, smartwatch, and gaming headphones on EMI".

"Easy choice," Aarav said. "First one grows money. Second one just burns it".

"And that," Zara smiled, "is the mindset of smart borrowing".

Smart borrowing means thinking before spending. Plan your budget, ask the right questions, and borrow only what you can repay with confidence.

Rule 1: Borrow Only When You Must

Ananya wrote it clearly on the whiteboard: "**Need beats want**. Every time."

"Ask yourself," she said:

- *Is this urgent?*
- *Will it improve my life or income?*
- *Can I not do this without borrowing?*

"If the answer to most of these is no," Zara added, "you should wait or save up".

Rule 2: Compare Before You Commit

Rohan shared an example. "Two banks offer the same loan amount. One charges 10 percent interest, the other 12 percent. Over five years, the difference in total repayment is huge".

"Always check:
- *Interest rate*
- *Processing fees*
- *Repayment flexibility*
- *Hidden charges*" Ananya said.

"Treat loans like shopping" Kabir added. "Look for the best deal".

Rule 3: Know Your EMI Limit

"Never let your monthly EMIs cross more than 30 percent of your income" Zara explained. "It leaves room for emergencies".

"And always add a buffer" said Rohan. "What if your income drops or expenses go up?"

"Think long term" Aarav added. "Don't borrow today and regret it for three years".

Rule 4: Read Everything

Kabir groaned. "Fine print again?"

"Yes," said Ananya. "Always. Look for:
- *Prepayment charges*
- *Late payment penalties*
- *Extra conditions like mandatory insurance*

"Don't trust ads. Trust the documents" said Rohan.

"Also, keep copies of everything" Zara added. "You never know when you'll need them".

Rule 5: Avoid Emotional Borrowing

Aarav raised his hand. "What's that?"

"Borrowing because of peer pressure or FOMO" said Ananya. "Like getting a new phone just because your friends have one".

"Or taking a vacation loan because everyone is posting about theirs" Kabir added.

"Borrowing should be a logical decision" said Zara. "Not an emotional one".

Rule 6: Plan Repayment Before You Borrow

"Most people borrow first and think about how to repay later" said Rohan. "That's a mistake".

"Use a loan calculator" Zara said. "Make a plan. Know your monthly EMI. Set reminders".

"And have an emergency fund" Ananya added. "So one small setback doesn't ruin everything".

Quick Recap

Before they left, Ananya wrote the six golden rules on the board:

1. *Borrow only when needed*
2. *Compare loan options*
3. *Keep EMIs within your limit*
4. *Read all terms and documents*
5. *Don't borrow emotionally*
6. *Plan repayment in advance*

"Borrowing is a tool," Zara said. "But only if you know how to use it".

"Like driving a car," Rohan added. "Know the road, know the brakes".

The Piggy Bank Society left the library that day with not just knowledge, but a checklist. A way to stay smart in a world full of tempting loans.

Chapter 8

Should You Take the Loan?

The final meeting of the term had a different vibe. The Piggy Bank Society knew the drill by now - come with an open mind, leave with a sharper one. But today, there would be no new lesson. Instead, they were going to put everything they had learned into practice.

Ananya stood at the front of the room with three folded cards in her hand.

"Each of these is a loan scenario" she said. "Your job is to decide whether to take the loan or not. But more importantly, tell us why".

Kabir grinned. "Finally, a quiz I'm actually ready for".

Every loan decision is a balancing act. It's not just about what you want but what you truly need, and whether the timing is right

Scenario 1: The Flashy Phone

Aarav read the first card aloud. "You're in class 10. Your phone works fine, but a new model just launched with a better camera and more storage. It costs ₹28,000. You don't have the money, but the store offers 0 percent EMI for 12 months".

Rohan was the first to speak. "Nope. That's a want, not a need".

"Also, 0 percent EMI often hides processing fees or extra charges" said Ananya.

"Plus, by the time you finish paying, a newer phone will already be out" Kabir added.

Verdict: *Not worth it.*

Scenario 2: The Science Camp

Zara picked the second card. "You've been selected for an international science camp. Total cost is ₹80,000. Your parents can pay half. You consider a loan for the rest. Interest rate is 10 percent over one year".

"This is an opportunity" said Aarav. "It can help you learn, grow, maybe even earn more later".

"The loan is small, the interest is reasonable, and the benefit is long-term" said Rohan.

"Plus, it's for education" said Ananya. "Always a smart investment".

Verdict: *Worth it.*

Scenario 3: The Family Emergency

Kabir read the last card. "A close family member needs urgent medical treatment. The hospital needs ₹1,50,000 upfront. Your family has ₹50,000 in savings. The bank offers a personal loan for the rest at 12 percent interest".

"Immediate need. No other option. The loan makes sense" said Zara.

"This is why borrowing exists. To help during emergencies" said Ananya.

"You just need to plan repayment well" added Rohan.

Verdict: *Definitely yes.*

The Borrowing Filter

Ananya stood up and wrote a checklist on the board:

- *Is it a need or a want?*
- *Will it improve your future or earnings?*

- *Can you repay it comfortably?*
- *Is the cost of the loan reasonable?*
- *Are there hidden fees or conditions?*

"If you can check at least three of these confidently," she said, "you're making an informed decision."

"Otherwise, it's better to wait," said Zara.

Quick Recap

Rohan looked around the room. "We started thinking borrowing was just about getting money. But it's more like a commitment. A contract. A decision that affects your future".

"It's not just about what you buy" said Aarav. "It's about what you pay for it: both in money and in peace of mind."

"Borrow smart, not fast" said Kabir. "And definitely not to impress someone".

"Good decisions come from good thinking" said Ananya. "And good thinking needs knowledge. That's what we've built together".

The Piggy Bank Society smiled. They had come a long way from simple savings to the complex world of loans, credit, and responsibility.

UNDERSTANDING BANKS

Chapter 1

Welcome to the World of Banks

The Piggy Bank Society had returned older, wiser, and just as curious.

The school bell rang, echoing through the halls, and one by one the members gathered in their favorite hideout - the back corner of the school library. It wasn't fancy. A long table. Five mismatched chairs. A soft breeze from the rattling ceiling fan. But to them, it was the headquarters of every big idea.

Zara was already flipping through a dusty book on economics when Ananya walked in, followed closely by Kabir, Aarav, and Rohan.

"I brought snacks" Kabir announced proudly, holding up a packet of banana chips.

"I brought questions" Ananya said, raising an eyebrow. "Same energy".

Everyone chuckled. As the group settled in, Rohan pulled out a sheet of paper. Scribbled across it in bold letters was the day's topic:

Every loan decision is a balancing act. It's not just about what you want but what you truly need, and whether the timing is right

'WHERE DOES YOUR MONEY GO AFTER YOU GIVE IT TO THE BANK?'

Entering the World of Banks

"So" Aarav said, tearing open the chips, "I gave ₹500 to the bank last month. Where is it now? Sitting in a safe? Floating in space? Being turned into coins?!"

"Honestly, same question" Kabir said. "It's like the money disappears and the app just shows a number. Poof".

Zara grinned. "Not quite poof. But not too far from magic either. Banks don't just store your money. They use it".

"Wait" said Rohan, leaning forward. "You mean they do stuff with our money while we're not looking?"

"Exactly" Ananya nodded. "Banks are more like financial engines than lockers. They help money move - between people, businesses, and governments. That movement grows the economy".

What Exactly Is a Bank?

Kabir scribbled the word 'BANK' in big block letters on a notepad.

"So what even is a bank?" he asked.

"A bank is a place that accepts deposits from the public and gives out loans"

Zara explained. "It earns money by charging interest on those loans. Basically, it's a middleman for money".

"Kind of like how a library lends books" said Rohan. "You borrow, return, repeat".

"But with banks, if you don't return on time, you pay extra" Ananya added. "That's the interest. And if you do deposit money, you earn interest instead".

"Wait, so banks pay us for giving them money?" Aarav asked.

"Yup" Zara nodded. "Because they use that money to make more money".

Why Do Banks Even Exist?

"Imagine a world without banks" said Rohan. "No ATMs, no UPI, no safe place to keep your money".

"No car loans, no business loans, no savings interest" added Ananya.

"You'd probably be keeping your allowance under your pillow" Kabir said. "Which sounds cool until your little brother finds it".

Everyone laughed.

"But seriously" said Zara, "banks create **trust**. They keep our money safe, help us grow it, and make big things - like homes and companies - possible".

"And they're regulated by the **Reserve Bank of India** so they don't misuse that trust" Ananya added.

What Can You Do With a Bank Account?

The group listed it out on the whiteboard behind them:
- **Deposit money**
- **Withdraw cash** from ATMs or counters
- **Transfer funds** via UPI, NEFT, IMPS
- **Pay bills** automatically
- **Apply for loans**
- **Earn interest** on savings

"Basically" Zara said, "banks are like the Swiss Army knife of the financial world. One account. So many tools".

"Okay, but what's the catch?" Kabir asked. "Banks don't just do all this for free, right?"

"Bingo" said Rohan. "And that's what we'll talk about next week - **how banks make money**".

Quick Recap

Before packing up, Ananya recapped:
- A bank stores your money safely and helps it grow
- Banks lend money to others and charge interest
- Without banks, the economy would move a lot slower
- Banks are **trust-based systems** regulated by the RBI
- And they're way more than just lockers - they're the **engines of the economy**

As they zipped up their bags, Kabir looked thoughtful. "So basically, I'm not just saving money. I'm powering something".

The Piggy Bank Society left the library with a little more understanding and the kind of excitement that only comes from cracking open something important - like the world of banks.

Chapter 2

The Birth of Banking –
A Trip Through History

The next time the Piggy Bank Society gathered in the library, Rohan brought a prop. It was a clay pot with a lid.

"This" he said, placing it on the table with dramatic flair, "is a replica of what ancient Mesopotamians used to store money. Well, not money. Grains, silver, maybe goats. But you get the idea".

Kabir leaned in. "So you're telling me banking started with pots?"

"Pretty much" Zara laughed. "Today's topic is not just how banks work. It's about how they began".

"And how we went from bartering cows to tapping phones" said Ananya, flipping open her notebook. "Let's time-travel".

From barter to banks, money's journey is full of clever ideas, trusted records, and secure places…each one bringing us closer to how we save and spend today

Life Before Banks: Barter and Beads

"In the beginning, there was no money" Rohan began. "People exchanged goods directly. I give you wheat, you give me fish. That was the **barter system**".

"But barter had problems" Zara added. "What if I have apples but want shoes, and the shoemaker doesn't like apples?"

"That's called the *double coincidence of wants*" said Ananya. "And it's super inconvenient".

"So people started using things everyone valued" Aarav said. "Salt, shells, even cattle. These became **primitive money**".

"In India, people used **cowrie shells,** and in Africa, salt bricks were money" Rohan said. "It was all about mutual trust".

The First Bankers: Temples and Merchants

"Eventually" Ananya said, "people needed a safe place to store valuable stuff".

"Enter temples" Zara nodded. "In ancient Mesopotamia, temples acted like banks. You could store grain, gold, silver there".

"Even in ancient India, merchants and moneylenders acted as informal banks" Rohan added. "They'd write promissory notes and keep records".

"China had the earliest version of paper currency in the 7th century" Ananya said. "And in Italy, in the Middle Ages, merchants started lending money with interest".

"So that's where banking as a business began" Kabir said. "Not just storing money, but growing it".

The Medici Family and Modern Banking

"Now comes the Medici family" Zara said. "In 15th century **Florence**, they ran one of the first organized banks in Europe".

"They introduced *double-entry bookkeeping*" Ananya said. "That changed everything".

"It allowed bankers to track deposits, loans, and interest in a structured way" Rohan added. "It was the birth of modern accounting".

"And it spread across Europe" Aarav said. "France, the Netherlands, and England all built strong banking systems".

Banking Comes to India

"So when did banking officially start in India?" Kabir asked.

"The first modern bank in India was the **Bank of Hindustan**, founded in 1770 in Calcutta" Rohan said.

"Then came the **Bank of Bengal, Bank of Bombay, and Bank of Madras**" Ananya added. "Together, they were called the Presidency Banks".

"In 1921, they merged to form the **Imperial Bank of India**, which later became the **State Bank of India** in 1955" Zara said.

"SBI is like the grandparent of Indian banking" Aarav joked.

From Coins to QR Codes

"Over time, India's banking system expanded massively" Rohan said. "From a few colonial banks to nationalized banks, private banks, and now digital banks".

"Don't forget cooperative banks, payment banks, and small finance banks" Ananya added. "We'll dive into those later".

"It's amazing how we've gone from trading cattle to scanning QR codes" Zara said.

"And the common thread through it all?" Kabir asked.

"Trust" Ananya answered. "Banking has always been about trust. Whether you're giving your coins to a merchant or transferring money online".

Quick Recap

Zara summarized their time-traveling lesson:

- People started with **barter** and moved to objects of value as early money
- Temples and merchants acted as the first banks
- The **Medici family** laid the foundation for modern banking in Europe
- India's formal banking began in the late 1700s and evolved into today's SBI and beyond

"Banking is history in motion" Rohan said. "Every transaction today is part of a story that started thousands of years ago".

The Piggy Bank Society closed their notebooks, the past still swirling in their thoughts. From pots of silver to mobile apps, they now saw banking not just as a service, but a centuries-old story of evolution and trust.

Chapter 3

How Banks Make Money

The next afternoon, the library felt especially quiet, almost as if it knew the Piggy Bank Society was about to uncover a powerful secret. Rohan had brought a small whiteboard and had already drawn two stick figures labeled **"Saver" and "Borrower"**.

"Alright" he said, pointing to the figures, "here's you. You give money to the bank. And here's someone else. They take money from the bank. Question is, how does the bank make money from this?"

Kabir leaned back in his chair. "Easy. They charge people for borrowing, and they give us way less in return. I call it daylight robbery".

Everyone laughed, but Ananya raised a hand.

"Not robbery, Kabir. It's called **interest spread**. And it's how banks stay alive".

Banks don't just store your money - they help it grow.
And by lending wisely, they grow too

Deposits and Loans – The Core Cycle

Zara stood up and wrote two big words on the board: **Deposits and Loans.**

"When we put money in a savings account, the bank takes those funds and lends them out as loans" she said. "They pay us **interest** for keeping money, and they charge others **more interest** when lending it".

"So if I deposit ₹1,000 and get 3 percent interest, and they lend it to someone at 10 percent, the bank keeps the 7 percent difference?" Aarav asked.

"Exactly" said Ananya. "That's called the **Net Interest Margin**. It's how banks make most of their money".

"But wait" Kabir interrupted. "They don't give my exact ₹1,000 to someone, right?"

"Good catch" said Rohan. "Which brings us to something called **fractional reserve banking**".

Fractional Reserve Banking – Lending Without Running Dry

Zara drew a pyramid on the board.

"Banks don't keep all your money in a locker. They're only required to keep a **fraction** - maybe 4 to 10 percent - as reserves. The rest? They lend it out".

Kabir's eyes widened. "So if everyone went to withdraw their money at once…"

"That would be a **bank run**" Rohan said. "And yes, that's why regulation by the RBI is important. It ensures banks have enough to meet daily needs but still keep the economy moving".

"It's like a big trust game" Aarav muttered. "And we're all players".

Other Ways Banks Earn

"Apart from lending, banks earn from a bunch of other things" Ananya added. She listed them out on the board:

- **Account fees** – charges for not maintaining minimum balance
- **ATM charges** – after free transactions
- **Processing fees** – on loans and credit cards

- **Commissions** – for selling insurance or mutual funds
- **Forex** and **international transaction charges**

"I once got charged ₹250 for withdrawing cash from another bank's ATM" Kabir grumbled. "Felt like a fine for touching my own money".

"That's how banks turn services into revenue" Zara said. "Small charges across millions of customers add up to big earnings".

Risk and Reward – What Happens if People Don't Repay?

"Okay, so banks lend money and make money from interest" Aarav said. "But what if someone doesn't return the loan?"

"Then the loan becomes a **Non-Performing Asset or NPA**" Rohan said. "It means the bank is losing money".

"Too many NPAs, and the bank can get into serious trouble" Ananya said. "That's why they do background checks, ask for collateral, and follow credit scores".

"Like a report card for your financial behaviour" Zara added. "Which we'll get into later".

A Simple Simulation

"Let's say our school's canteen is a bank" Rohan said. "We each deposit ₹100. That's ₹500 total. The canteen lends ₹400 to a student who wants to buy ingredients to start a snack stall".

"If the stall does well, the student repays ₹440" said Zara. "The canteen gives us back ₹102 each and keeps the rest as profit".

"But if the stall fails" Ananya continued, "and the student only returns ₹200, then the canteen takes a loss".

"Which means our returns drop or the canteen needs help" Aarav said. "Makes sense why banks play it safe".

A Quick Recap

Ananya summarized:
- Banks earn mainly through interest on loans
- They pay savers less and charge borrowers more
- Only a fraction of your deposit is kept in cash
- Banks also earn from service charges and commissions
- If many loans go bad, banks can fail

"So banking isn't just about holding money" Zara said. "It's about moving it, managing it, and making more of it".

"And next time" said Kabir, "we see a bank ad offering 'free everything,' we'll know what's really going on".

The Piggy Bank Society closed their notebooks, each member now seeing banks as clever machines - turning rupees into returns, and trust into transactions.

Chapter 4

Types of Banks

The library felt extra cozy that day, as if it knew the Piggy Bank Society was about to unpack another big layer of the financial world. Rohan had taken over one end of the whiteboard and had written in bold letters:

"ALL BANKS ARE NOT THE SAME"

Kabir raised an eyebrow. "I thought banks were just… banks. You know, you go in, you put your money in, you get it out".

"Same here" said Aarav. "SBI, ICICI, Axis - they all kind of look and feel the same".

"Not really" Zara said, already flipping through her notes.

"There are different types of banks, each doing very different things. Some are for us. Some are for businesses. Some are for farmers. Some don't even have branches".

"Let's sort them out" said Ananya. "One by one".

*Banks come in many types - each with a special role.
Knowing the difference helps you make better money
decisions*

Commercial Banks – The Ones We All Know

Ananya began. "These are the banks most of us use. They offer savings accounts, give loans, issue credit cards, and help us pay bills".

"Like **SBI, HDFC, ICICI, Axis**" said Rohan.

"Exactly" Zara said. "These are commercial banks. They work with individuals, small businesses, and even big corporations".

"And they're regulated by the Reserve Bank of India, just like all others" Ananya added.

"These are the banks you find in shopping malls, on your street, and on every UPI app" Kabir said. "They're the public face of banking".

Cooperative Banks – The People's Banks

"Next up" said Zara, "cooperative banks. These are **banks started by communities**. Think farmers, shopkeepers, or workers who pool their resources to help each other".

"They're smaller and more local" Rohan said. "And they're meant to be people-first".

"Do they give loans too?" Aarav asked.

"Absolutely" Ananya nodded.

"Especially to people in villages or small towns who may not get loans easily from commercial banks".

"Cool" Kabir said. "Like the original team-up".

Payments Banks – Digital and Light

"Now let's get techy" Zara said. "Payments banks are new-age banks. **They mostly exist online.** No big buildings. No cash counters".

"Like **Paytm Payments Bank, Airtel Payments Bank**" Rohan added.

"You can deposit money, pay bills, and use UPI" said Ananya. "But you **can't** take loans or keep more than ₹2 lakh in them".

"Useful for quick transactions" said Aarav. "But not for saving big amounts".

Small Finance Banks – Banking the Underserved

"These are really cool" Ananya said. "Small Finance Banks were started to bring banking to people who've never had access to it".

"Like **farmers, small traders, daily wage earners**" Zara added.

"Some names you might've heard - **AU Small Finance Bank, Ujjivan, Jana**" said Rohan.

"They do everything a normal bank does - savings, loans, deposits - but their goal is inclusion" Ananya explained.

Development Banks – Building the Nation

"These are not for us" Kabir said, dramatically. "They are for India".

Everyone laughed.

"But he's right" Zara said. "Development banks like **NABARD, SIDBI, and EXIM** Bank don't serve individuals. They give big loans to projects that help the economy - like building roads, helping farmers, or supporting small industries".

"They're like the backstage crew" said Aarav. "You don't see them, but they make the show happen".

The Central Bank – The Boss of All Banks

"Last but not least" said Rohan. "The Reserve Bank of India, or RBI".

"The RBI prints our currency, controls inflation, sets interest rates, and keeps banks in check" Ananya added.

"If commercial banks are the players" Zara said, "RBI is the referee, coach, and manager rolled into one"

"They also rescue banks when things go wrong" Kabir said. "Like they did with Yes Bank in 2020".

Visual Recap on the Whiteboard

The group listed everything out:

- **Commercial Banks** – For individuals and businesses (SBI, HDFC, etc.)
- **Cooperative Banks** – Local, member-owned, people-first
- **Payments Banks** – Mobile-based, limited features

- **Small Finance Banks** – Serve the underserved
- **Development Banks** – Fund large-scale national projects
- **RBI** – Regulates and manages the entire system

"Each bank has a different purpose" said Zara. "And together, they form the entire financial backbone of the country".

"Which means the next time someone says 'bank,' we should ask - what kind?" said Ananya.

"Exactly" Rohan smiled. "Because not all banks wear the same uniform".

The Piggy Bank Society packed up their things, now able to see the banking system not as a single building, but a network of institutions, each playing a different role in India's growth.

Chapter 5

Digital Banking and the Future of Money

The library was buzzing with energy, not because of noise, but because everyone in the Piggy Bank Society was on their phones. This time, they weren't playing games or checking messages - they were all exploring their banking apps.

"You know" Aarav said, without looking up, "I haven't visited an actual bank branch in… maybe ever. Everything I do with money happens on my phone".

"Same here" said Kabir. "From paying for pani puri to transferring my allowance to savings - it's all UPI now".

"That's why today" Zara said, setting down her tablet, "we talk about the future of banking, which - spoiler alert - is already here".

Banking is no longer just a place, it's something you can carry in your pocket. The future is already here, and it's digital

From Passbooks to Phone Screens

"Banking used to mean going to a branch, filling out forms, and waiting in lines" Rohan said. "But now, you can open an account, transfer money, and pay bills without stepping out of your house".

"And India is leading the charge in this" Ananya added. "We're one of the top countries when it comes to **digital payments**".

UPI – India's Digital Revolution

"Let's start with the star of the show - UPI, or **Unified Payments Interface**" said Zara.

"Launched in 2016 by the NPCI, it allows money transfers between bank accounts instantly using a phone".

"No IFSC codes. No waiting. Just a UPI ID or a phone number" said Aarav.

"And it works 24x7 - even at 3 a.m". Kabir added.

"In fact" said Ananya, "India processed over **10 billion UPI transactions in a single month.** That's more than most countries combined".

"UPI has made digital banking accessible to everyone - from students to street vendors" Rohan said.

Digital Wallets and Neo-Banks

"So what's the difference between a **digital wallet and a bank app**?" Aarav asked.

"Good question" said Ananya. "A wallet like **Paytm** stores prepaid money. You load ₹500, and then spend it. A bank app, like **SBI YONO**, is linked directly to your account".

"And what about neo-banks?" Kabir asked.

"Neo-banks are like fully digital banks without any physical branches" Zara explained. "They partner with licensed banks and offer services through apps. Examples include Jupiter and Fi".

"They're fast, smart, and app-based - but still safe because they're tied to regular banks" said Rohan.

FinTech – Banking Without Borders

"FinTech means Financial Technology" Ananya said. "It refers to startups that offer financial services using technology".

"Like Zerodha for investing, PhonePe for payments, or KreditBee for small loans" Zara added.

"Even budgeting apps are FinTech" Kabir said. "I use one to track my spending. And it roasts me every time I buy too many snacks".

Everyone laughed.

"But seriously" said Rohan, "FinTech is making banking faster, more personal, and more accessible".

Is It Safe? The Cyber Side of Banking

"Digital banking sounds awesome" Aarav said. "But is it safe?"

"Great point" said Ananya. "Digital banking brings risks like **phishing, fraudulent apps, and data theft**".

"That's why we need to:

- Use strong passwords
- Avoid public Wi-Fi for transactions
- Never share OTPs
- Only use trusted apps from official stores" Zara explained.

"And remember" Rohan added, "banks never ask for your PIN or password over a call or message".

Quick Recap

Zara listed the key takeaways:

- Digital banking makes transactions faster and easier
- UPI has made India a global leader in cashless payments
- Wallets, bank apps, and neo-banks are changing how we manage money
- FinTech is expanding access to banking
- But we must always stay safe online

"Money used to be stored in lockers" said Ananya. "Now it lives in the cloud".

"And if we're smart about it" Kabir said, "we can use that cloud to fly".

The group grinned, their screens glowing softly in the afternoon light. The future of money wasn't just coming - it was already in their pockets.

Chapter 6

What Happens
When a Bank Fails?

That week, the library felt a little heavier. Kabir walked in holding a newspaper.

"Guys, check this out" he said, spreading it open on the table. "A bank almost shut down last year. People were lining up outside, panicking".

"Yeah" Zara nodded. "That was Yes Bank in 2020. The RBI had to step in".

"Banks can actually fail?" Aarav asked, surprised. "Like, shut down completely?"

"They can" Ananya said. "And when they do, it affects millions of people. But the system is designed to stop things from getting that bad".

Even when banks stumble, systems are in place to protect your money. Knowing this makes you a smarter, calmer saver

Why Do Banks Fail?

Rohan picked up a marker and began writing on the whiteboard.

"Here are a few reasons why banks fail:
- **Too many bad loans (called NPAs)**
- **Poor management**
- **Sudden loss of customer trust**
- **Economic slowdowns**"

"Let's say a bank gives loans to five companies" Zara said. "And all five go bankrupt. That's a huge loss".

"And if customers start withdrawing money in fear, it becomes worse" Ananya added. "That's called a bank run".

"Like musical chairs" Kabir said. "If too many people grab their money at once, there's not enough left".

What Is a Bank Run?

"A bank run happens when people think the bank might collapse" Rohan explained. "So everyone rushes to withdraw their money. But banks only keep a small percentage of deposits in cash".

"Because of fractional reserve banking" Aarav remembered.

"Exactly" Zara nodded. "If too many people withdraw at once, the bank can't keep up".

"It's like panic causing more panic" Kabir said.

The RBI to the Rescue

"Here's where the Reserve Bank of India steps in" Ananya said. "It acts like a safety net".

Zara wrote on the board:

- RBI can **restrict withdrawals temporarily**
- It can **provide emergency funds**
- It can help **merge** the failing bank with a stronger one
- It can **take control** of the bank's management

"That's what happened with Yes Bank" Rohan said. "The RBI brought in SBI to invest and stabilise the bank".

Is My Money Safe?

"So if a bank fails, do we lose all our money?" Aarav asked.

"No" said Zara. "Thanks to something called the **DICGC - Deposit Insurance and Credit Guarantee Corporation**".

"Every depositor is **insured up to ₹5 lakh** per bank" Ananya explained.

"So if I have ₹4 lakh in one bank, it's safe. But if I have ₹10 lakh, only ₹5 lakh is guaranteed?" Kabir asked.

"Right" said Rohan. "That's why it's smart to spread your money across banks if you have large savings".

Global Bank Failures

"This isn't just an Indian problem" Zara said."Banks have failed across the world"

"Like **Lehman Brothers in 2008**" Rohan added. "That collapse triggered a global financial crisis".

"More recently, **Silicon Valley Bank** failed in the US" said Ananya. "They put too much money in long-term bonds, and when people rushed to withdraw, they couldn't keep up".

"Even big banks can fall" Kabir said. "That's scary".

"Which is why regulations are so important" Ananya replied. "The system needs rules, and someone to enforce them".

Quick Recap

Ananya summarised:

- Banks can fail due to bad loans, mismanagement, or panic
- A bank run happens when everyone tries to withdraw at once
- The RBI protects the banking system by stepping in
- Deposits up to ₹5 lakh are insured by DICGC
- Spreading money across banks can reduce risk

"Banking works on trust" Zara said. "And when that trust breaks, the whole system shakes".

"But with the right safety nets" Rohan said, "most people stay protected".

The Piggy Bank Society packed up slowly, the mood thoughtful. They had uncovered the darker side of banking - not to fear it, but to understand it.

Because being money-wise meant knowing the risks, too.

Chapter 7

Money Safety –
How to Be a Smart Banker

After last week's serious discussion about failing banks, the Piggy Bank Society decided it was time for some **defensive play.**

"We've talked about how banks make money and even how they can fail" Ananya said, settling into her chair. "Now let's talk about how we can stay safe with our money".

Zara pulled out a colourful folder and flipped it open. "Welcome to your crash course in **Banking Safety 101**".

Choose Your Bank Wisely

"First things first" said Rohan. "Not all banks are equally safe".

"Always go for banks that are regulated by the RBI and insured under DICGC" Zara added.

Being a smart banker means protecting what you have earned - online, offline and everywhere in between

"Stick to trusted names" Ananya said. "And check their reputation, customer service, and financial health if you're opening a fixed deposit".

"If a bank promises super high returns, be careful" Aarav said. "It might be too good to be true".

Read the Fine Print

"Opening an account feels easy" said Kabir. "But there's always that 3-page terms and conditions doc".

"Which no one reads" Rohan groaned.

"Well, we should" Zara said firmly. "Check things like:

- Minimum balance requirement
- ATM withdrawal limits
- SMS and debit card charges
- Penalty for early withdrawal on FDs"

"You might be losing money without knowing it" said Ananya.

Digital Safety – Don't Be the Weak Link

"Digital banking is great" said Rohan. "But only if we stay smart".

Zara listed some golden rules:
- Never share **PIN, password, or OTP**
- Don't click on **suspicious links** or download unverified apps
- Use **strong passwords** and change them regularly
- Always use **secure internet** - no banking on public Wi-Fi

"And if you get a call saying 'I'm from your bank,' hang up and call the official number" Kabir added.

"Banks never ask for sensitive info on calls or messages" Aarav said. "That's **Phishing** 101".

Keep Track of Your Transactions

"Make it a habit to check your balance and transactions regularly" said Ananya.

"Even a small wrong charge should be flagged immediately" Zara added. "It could be a mistake - or fraud".

"And set up alerts" Rohan said. "Get notified every time money moves".

"Knowledge is power" Aarav nodded. "Especially when it's your money".

Avoid Emotional Spending and Impulse Traps

"Safety isn't just about tech" said Kabir. "It's also about self-control".

"Don't fall for offers like 'Buy now, pay later' without checking the details" said Zara.

"Make a budget. Set limits" Ananya added. "Think before you tap".

"If you need a moment to decide, just say, 'Let me check with my Piggy Bank Society,'" Aarav said, laughing.

Spread Your Risk

"If you're saving a large amount" Rohan said, "don't keep it all in one place".

"Open accounts in different banks" Ananya added. "Remember, DICGC only insures up to ₹5 lakh per person / bank".

"It's like not putting all your pani puris in one plate" Kabir joked. "One falls, you still have backups".

Quick Recap

"We trust banks with our hard-earned money" said Ananya. "Let's make sure we're smart enough to protect it".

"Being financially wise isn't just about earning or saving" Rohan added. "It's about staying alert".

The group packed up, feeling more in control than ever. The Piggy Bank Society wasn't just learning finance - they were building habits for life.

And next week, they would wrap it all up with one final debate - Do we even need banks anymore?

Chapter 8

Do We Even Need Banks?

The Piggy Bank Society gathered one last time for the term. It had been weeks of learning, debating, and understanding the mysterious world of banking. But today's topic felt different. It was more of a challenge than a lesson.

"Okay" Zara said, standing at the front of the group. "We've spent all this time learning about banks. But what if I told you some people think we don't need banks anymore?"

Kabir raised an eyebrow. "Like, just cancel them?"

"Well" Ananya said, "with all the digital wallets, UPI apps, peer-to-peer payment platforms, and even crypto... people are asking, do we still need traditional banks?"

"Let's debate it" Rohan said. "One side argues for banks. The other side, against".

The team split up, grabbing notebooks and sketching out their arguments.

In a world of new technology, banks still play an old but important role. The future might be a mix of both trust and tech

The Case for Banks

Rohan took the floor. "Let's start with the basics. Banks give:

- Safe storage for money
- Access to loans
- Fixed deposits for savings
- Government-backed security
- Legal documentation and proof of funds"

"They're essential for getting things like home loans, education loans, business funding" Zara added.

"And they're heavily regulated, which adds trust".

"And during emergencies or failures, the RBI can step in" Ananya said. "That kind of backup doesn't exist with digital wallets or crypto".

"Also" Rohan continued, "banks reach remote parts of India with financial inclusion programs. Private FinTechs may not do that".

The Case Against Banks

Kabir cleared his throat dramatically. "Now, let me tell you why people are getting tired of banks".

He listed:
- High service fees
- Complex documentation
- Slow processing for loans
- Hidden charges
- Lack of flexibility

"UPI is free, instant, and always available" Aarav added. "I can split lunch bills with a tap. No bank form required".

"Neo-banks and FinTech apps offer smart budgeting tools, better user experience, and fast support" said Kabir. "They feel like they're made for us, not our grandparents".

"And with crypto and blockchain" Aarav added, "some people are creating financial systems without any middlemen".

So... What's the Middle Ground?

After both sides finished, Ananya stood up.

"Maybe it's not about banks vs. apps. Maybe it's about evolution" she said.

"Banks are changing" Zara agreed.

"Many offer great digital services now. It's not either-or. It's both".

"The future of finance will probably have both traditional banks and modern tools" Rohan said. "Each solving different problems".

"And whatever the tool" Aarav added, "we'll still need trust, safety, and responsibility".

Final Thoughts

Kabir raised his hand. "So we don't need banks the way they used to be. But we still need the functions they provide".

"Well said" Ananya nodded. "It's not about who or what we use. It's about using it smartly".

The Piggy Bank Society packed their bags slowly. This wasn't the end of their journey - just the start of a new phase.

They weren't just banking literate. They were financially curious, cautious, and confident.

As they left the library, Aarav said, "Okay but just for fun... should we start our own Piggy Bank Society App?"

Everyone laughed.

And maybe, just maybe, that idea would one day become real.

SEASON 6

INSURANCE BASICS

Chapter 1

What If...? The World of Risk and Protection

It was a windy afternoon at school and the library windows were rattling just enough to give the day a dramatic vibe. The Piggy Bank Society had assembled as usual, notebooks open, snacks in hand.

Kabir had just finished his sandwich when he asked, "What if a tree falls on our school bus? Like randomly?"

"Or what if your bicycle gets stolen from outside the tuition center?" added Aarav.

"Or someone in your family suddenly has to go to the hospital?" said Zara.

Ananya nodded. "Exactly the right kind of thinking. Welcome to the world of 'what ifs'. And today, we start talking

"Yes" said Ananya. "It's like carrying an umbrella in your bag. You might not need it, but when it rains, you'll be glad you had it".

Risk is everywhere but protection is possible. Planning ahead helps turn surprises into manageable moments

Everyday Risks We Don't Think About

Aarav listed some risks they all faced without even realising:

- Falling ill and needing expensive hospital care
- A scooter getting into a minor accident
- Travel delays or baggage loss
- Damage to your home during heavy rains

"And these things cost money to fix" said Zara. "Sometimes a lot of money".

"Which not every family can afford on short notice" said Rohan.

"That's why we have insurance" said Ananya. "To avoid turning a bad situation into a financial crisis".

The Core Idea: Shared Risk

Rohan stood up and used a marker to draw a circle.

"Imagine one hundred people each pay a small amount into a common fund. If something bad happens to one person, the fund helps them recover".

"That way, the risk is shared" said Ananya. "And no one person has to carry the full weight alone".

"It's like everyone chipping in to help their neighbor" said Aarav. "But in a system that's organized and fair".

What Insurance Isn't

Kabir asked, "Is insurance like saving money?"

"Not exactly" said Zara. "When you save, the money is always yours. With insurance, the money helps only if the event happens. Otherwise, it stays with the company".

"So *if nothing goes wrong, you 'lose' the premium*?" Kabir asked.

"Think of it this way" said Rohan. "Would you rather never fall sick and not use the money, or fall sick and be thankful insurance was there?"

Kabir nodded slowly. "Okay, that makes sense".

Why Kids Should Learn About This

"You might think insurance is only for grown-ups" said Ananya. "But it's everywhere. Your school trip might have group travel insurance. Your parents may have health insurance. Even your house and phone can be insured".

"And someday, when you earn your own money" said Zara, "you'll want to know how to protect it".

"Plus" said Aarav, "insurance companies are big employers. You could even work in the insurance sector one day".

"Or create a cool new insurance app" added Rohan.

Quick Recap

Zara wrapped up the session with the following pointers:
- Life has risks that we can't always predict
- Insurance helps protect us from financial loss when things go wrong
- The idea is based on shared risk and collective support

- It is not the same as savings
- Knowing about insurance early helps build smart financial habits

"So next time you hear someone mention a premium or a policy" said Ananya, "you'll know they're talking about protection, not just paperwork".

"And next" said Rohan, "we'll crack open how insurance actually works. What's a claim? What's coverage? Let's decode the system".

The Piggy Bank Society left the library that day a little more thoughtful, and a lot more prepared for life's what ifs.

Chapter 2

What Is Insurance and How Does It Work?

The Piggy Bank Society met in their usual spot, and this time Zara brought a strange-looking file folder.

"My dad's insurance file" she said, placing it on the table. "It's thick. And full of words I don't understand".

"Perfect" said Ananya. "Because today, we're going to break down what insurance really is. And make sense of all that jargon".

Insurance in Simple Words

Rohan stood up and wrote on the board:

Insurance = Paying a small amount regularly to protect against a big loss later.

Insurance is about sharing risk. When everyone chips in a little, it helps protect anyone who faces a big loss

"Let's say you buy a cycle for ₹10,000" he said. "You pay ₹500 a year to insure it. If it gets stolen or damaged, the insurance company pays to repair or replace it".

"You don't get the ₹500 back" said Ananya, "but you don't have to pay ₹10,000 again either".

"So it's like a financial safety net" added Aarav.

Key Insurance Words to Know

Zara opened the file and picked out a few common terms.

- **Premium** – The amount you pay to the insurance company.
- **Policy** – The contract between you and the insurer.
- **Claim** – The request you make when something bad happens.
- **Coverage** – The total protection the policy offers.
- **Beneficiary** – The person who receives the insurance money.
- **Deductible** – The small part of the cost you pay before the insurance kicks in.

"Knowing these words helps you understand what you're buying" said Ananya.

A Real-Life Example: Cycle Insurance

Rohan gave a scenario:
- Kabir buys a new cycle.
- He pays ₹500 every year as premium.
- One day, the cycle gets stolen.
- He files a claim with the insurance company.
- After checking, they pay him ₹9,000 because ₹1,000 is the deductible.

"So Kabir only loses ₹1,000 instead of ₹10,000" said Aarav.

"That's insurance working exactly as it should" said Zara.

Why Not Just Save Instead?

Kabir raised a hand. "But what if I just save the ₹500 every year instead of giving it to an insurance company?"

"Great question" said Ananya. "Let's say nothing happens for four years. You'll have ₹2,000 saved. But if something happens in year five, and you lose ₹10,000, your savings won't be enough".

"That's the thing" said Rohan. "Insurance protects you even before you've saved enough".

"And it covers risks that could wipe out years of savings" added Zara.

How Insurance Companies Make Money

"Wait" Kabir said. "If they keep paying people, how do insurance companies survive?"

"They rely on probability" said Ananya. "Only a few people out of many actually make claims each year".

"They collect small premiums from everyone, but only pay out when necessary" said Aarav.

"And they invest the money they collect" added Rohan. "That helps them earn more".

Trust and the Fine Print

Zara held up the policy document. "Always read the fine print. Not everything is covered. There are terms and conditions".

"Like your insurance might not pay if the cycle wasn't locked" said Ananya. "Or if you don't file the claim properly".

"So trust is important, but so is understanding what you're signing up for" said Rohan.

Quick Recap

Ananya summarised:

- Insurance is a way to protect against big financial losses
- You pay a premium in exchange for coverage
- When something happens, you file a claim and receive help
- Insurance is different from saving - it gives protection from the start
- Always understand the terms before buying a policy

"Now that we know how it works" said Zara, "let's dive into the different types of insurance people in India actually use".

The Piggy Bank Society packed up, feeling much more confident. Next time someone in their family talked about premiums or claims, they wouldn't just nod - they'd understand.

Chapter 3

Types of Insurance in India

The Piggy Bank Society met on a cloudy Wednesday afternoon, and this time Rohan walked in with a big cardboard chart.

"I made a tree" he said proudly. "Not for biology class. For insurance".

The chart had "Insurance" written at the top, and branches going into different categories: life, health, motor, travel, crop, and home.

"Today, we're going to explore each of these branches" said Ananya. "Because insurance isn't one-size-fits-all. Different risks need different protection".

Insurance isn't one-size-fits-all. From health to crops, each type exists to protect what matters most to different people

Life Insurance

"Let's start with life insurance" said Rohan. *"It gives money to your family if something happens to the person insured"*.

Kabir asked, "Like if someone passes away?"

"Yes" said Zara. "Life insurance is about protecting the people who depend on you".

Ananya explained two types:

- **Term Insurance** – Pure protection. If the person dies during the term, the family gets money. If not, nothing is returned.
- **Endowment and ULIP Plans** – These are part insurance, part savings or investment. You get some money even if nothing happens.

"Most experts say term insurance is best if you want real protection" said Aarav.

Health Insurance

"Health insurance covers medical expenses" said Ananya. "Hospitals, surgeries, medicines".

Rohan listed some types:

- **Individual Plans** – Covers one person
- **Family Floater** – Covers all members under one plan

- **Critical Illness Plans** – Covers specific illnesses like cancer or heart disease
- **Government Schemes** – Like Ayushman Bharat for low-income families

"My cousin was in hospital for two weeks" said Kabir. "The insurance paid over ₹1.5 lakh. They only paid ₹20,000".

"That's the power of health insurance" said Ananya.

Motor Insurance

"Every vehicle on the road needs insurance" said Aarav.

"Motor insurance is not optional" added Zara. "It's mandatory in India".

Rohan explained:

- **Third-Party Insurance** – Covers damage caused to others. Required by law.
- **Comprehensive Insurance** – Covers your own vehicle as well as others' damage

"Without it, even a small accident could cost you thousands" said Ananya.

Travel Insurance

"What if your luggage gets lost during a flight?" asked Kabir.

"Travel insurance helps" said Zara. "It *covers lost baggage, flight cancellations, even emergency hospital care abroad*".

"It's useful for international trips" said Aarav. "Especially for students going abroad".

Home Insurance

"Your house is probably the most valuable thing your family owns" said Rohan.

Home insurance protects against:

- *Fire, floods, and natural disasters*
- *Theft or burglary*
- *Damage to property or belongings*

"Most people forget this" said Ananya. "But one big event could destroy years of savings".

Crop Insurance

"In rural India, crops are everything" said Zara.

"Imagine a flood or drought destroying an entire season's work" added Aarav.

"That's why we have *PMFBY – Pradhan Mantri Fasal Bima Yojana*" said Ananya. "It helps farmers recover from crop losses".

"Even weather and pest damage are covered" said Rohan.

Choosing the Right Insurance

Ananya listed tips on the board:

- Understand your needs and risks
- Start with essentials: health and term life insurance
- Use government schemes where eligible\
- Compare policies and premiums before buying

"Insurance is not about fear" said Zara. "It's about being ready".

Quick Recap

Before leaving, Aarav summarised:

- Life insurance protects your family's future
- Health insurance covers expensive medical costs
- Motor insurance is mandatory and protects you on the road
- Travel insurance helps with unexpected issues on trips
- Home insurance protects your property
- Crop insurance supports farmers after losses

"Now that we know the types" said Ananya, "next up is the team that watches over insurance companies in India: the IRDAI".

The Piggy Bank Society packed up, feeling like financial explorers who had just mapped out a new territory. Insurance wasn't a mystery anymore. It was a toolkit for life.

Chapter 4

The Role of IRDAI – The Insurance Watchdog

When the Piggy Bank Society gathered again, Ananya had drawn a cartoon of a big, serious-looking watchdog with the letters IRDAI on its collar.

Kabir laughed. "Is that the dog that barks at fake insurance agents?"

"In a way, yes" said Zara. "IRDAI is the reason insurance companies in India behave. *It makes sure they play fair and protect people*".

What Is IRDAI?

Rohan wrote it on the board: **Insurance Regulatory and Development Authority of India.**

"It was set up in 1999" said Ananya. "And it regulates the entire insurance sector".

The IRDAI acts like a referee for insurance companies - ensuring they're fair, transparent, and protect the rights of policyholders

"Think of it as the RBI of insurance" added Aarav. "It gives licenses, checks rules, and ensures companies stay honest".

Why Do We Need a Watchdog?

"Imagine if anyone could start an insurance company" said Zara. "They collect money and disappear. Total chaos".

Kabir nodded. "Or what if they say they'll pay for treatment, and then don't?"

"That's why IRDAI steps in" said Ananya. "It protects policyholders - the people who buy insurance".

What IRDAI Does

Rohan listed out IRDAI's key responsibilities:

- Licensing insurance companies and agents
- Setting rules for policies, premiums, and claims
- Monitoring performance of insurers
- Handling complaints from customers
- Educating people through awareness campaigns

"It also sets limits" said Zara. "Like how much commission agents can earn, or what information must be disclosed to customers".

"And it runs a website where you can compare policies" added Ananya.

Fighting Insurance Frauds

Kabir raised his hand. "What about frauds?"

"IRDAI takes action" said Rohan. *"If a company breaks rules, it can be fined or shut down".*

"Like if they reject claims unfairly or mislead customers" said Aarav.

"It also makes companies maintain solvency margins" said Zara. "That means they must have enough money to pay claims".

The Grievance System

Ananya showed a chart of steps:
- File a complaint with the insurance company
- If unresolved, go to **IRDAI's Integrated Grievance Management System (IGMS)**
- If still unresolved, go to the Insurance Ombudsman

"There's even a toll-free number and email ID" said Zara.

"So help is always available" said Kabir. "Good to know".

IRDAI and Innovation

"IRDAI also encourages **InsurTech**" said Rohan. "That's tech-powered insurance".

"Like apps for instant policy purchase, AI-based claim processing, and chatbots for customer support" said Aarav.

"And it creates a sandbox" said Ananya. "*A safe space for new insurance ideas to be tested before launching widely*".

Quick Recap

Before heading out, Zara summarised:

- IRDAI is the regulatory body for insurance in India
- It gives licenses, monitors companies, and protects customers
- It ensures fair play, prevents fraud, and handles complaints
- It also encourages innovation and digital tools

"Without IRDAI, insurance in India would be confusing and risky" said Rohan.

"And next" said Ananya, "we get into the details of life and health insurance - two of the most important kinds people rely on".

The Piggy Bank Society left that day feeling safer - not just because of insurance, but because someone was watching over it too.

Chapter 5

Decoding Life and Health Insurance

The library buzzed with a different energy that day. Kabir walked in carrying a small envelope.

"My parents just got a letter from their life insurance company. It had words like **term plan and policy maturity**. I didn't get half of it".

"Well then" said Zara, "today's chapter is going to help make all that crystal clear".

Why Life and Health Insurance Matter Most

"Out of all the types of insurance we've talked about" said Ananya, "life and health insurance are the most essential".

"Because they deal with people, not just things" added Rohan.

Life and health insurance aren't just paperwork - they're peace of mind, protecting your today and securing your tomorrow

"Exactly" said Zara. "They protect families from big emotional and financial shocks".

Understanding Life Insurance

Ananya drew a chart on the board and explained two major categories:

1. **Term Insurance:**
   - Simple, affordable
   - Fixed duration (like 10, 20, 30 years)
   - If the person dies during the term, the nominee gets the money
   - No money returned if nothing happens

2. **Endowment and ULIP Plans:**
   - Combine insurance with savings or investments
   - Higher premium
   - Some money is returned at the end of the term

"Term plans are best if your goal is just protection" said Zara. "The other types are useful if you also want savings or returns".

"And the person who receives the money is called **the nominee or beneficiary**" added Aarav.

Understanding Health Insurance

"Health insurance covers medical expenses" said Rohan. "That includes hospital stays, surgeries, medicines, and more".

Zara listed popular types:

- **Individual Plans** – For one person
- **Family Floater** – Covers the entire family under one policy
- **Critical Illness Plans** – Covers specific diseases like cancer, stroke, etc.
- **Top-up Plans** – Extra coverage beyond your basic policy

"There are also group health plans from employers" said Ananya. "And government schemes like **Ayushman Bharat**".

Key Terms You Should Know

Ananya pulled out a few flashcards:

- **Sum Insured**: The maximum amount the insurer will pay
- **Cashless Facility**: Hospital bills are settled directly by the insurer
- **Network Hospital**: A hospital that's tied up with the insurer
- **Pre-existing Illness**: Illnesses you had before buying the policy

- **Waiting Period:** Time before certain diseases are covered

"Understanding these terms is important before buying any health plan" said Rohan.

A Hospital Bill Breakdown

Kabir looked curious. "How much does it actually cost if someone's hospitalised?"
Aarav shared a made-up example:

- Surgery cost: ₹60,000
- Room charges: ₹10,000
- Medicines: ₹5,000
- Tests: ₹7,000
- Total: ₹82,000

"If you have insurance with cashless cover, most of this is paid directly by the insurer" said Zara.

"But you might still pay a small part if there's a room rent limit or non-covered items" added Ananya.

Claims in Life vs. Health Insurance

"In life insurance, the claim is made by the nominee after the policyholder passes away" said Rohan.

"In health insurance, the claim is made when someone falls ill or is admitted to the hospital" said Aarav.

"Both need proper documents" said Zara. "Like hospital bills, ID proof, and the insurance policy".

What Happens if You Don't Have Insurance?

Ananya posed a serious question. "Imagine paying ₹2 lakh from your savings for a medical emergency".

"It could wipe out your savings" said Rohan.

"That's why insurance is not a luxury. It's a must" said Zara.

Quick Recap

Before wrapping up, Ananya summarised:

- Life insurance protects families from financial loss due to death
- Health insurance covers the rising cost of medical treatment
- Term plans are affordable and focused on protection

- Health policies differ based on need and budget
- Claims must be filed properly with supporting documents

"Now that we've understood life and health insurance" said Zara, "next, we'll see what happens when things actually go wrong - and how to file a claim".

The Piggy Bank Society packed up, this time feeling more grown-up than usual. Understanding insurance wasn't just for adults - it was a skill for life.

Chapter 6

When Things Go Wrong – Filing a Claim

The library had a more serious tone that day. Kabir looked unusually quiet as he said, "My neighbour's car was hit last week. They had insurance, but the claim process seemed super complicated. Forms, photos, and so many calls".

"That's actually very common" said Zara. "Filing a claim is where people often get stuck. But it's not so bad if you know what to expect".

What is A Claim?

Ananya started by defining it: *"A claim is when you officially ask your insurance company to pay for a loss covered under your policy"*.

"So you're saying, 'I paid my premium. Now something went wrong. Please help me out,'" said Rohan.

"Exactly" said Ananya. "But for that, you need to follow certain steps".

Insurance helps you bounce back when life doesn't go as planned. A proper claim process makes sure help reaches the right hands at the right time.

Steps to File a Claim

Zara listed the typical process:

1. Inform the insurer immediately
2. Fill out the claim form
3. Submit required documents
4. Get a surveyor or inspection (if needed)
5. Wait for claim approval and payment

"Timing is important" said Aarav. "The sooner you inform them, the smoother it goes".

Documents You Might Need

Rohan pulled up a quick checklist for different types of insurance:

For Health Insurance:
- Hospital bills and discharge summary
- Doctor's prescription
- Tests and reports
- Insurance policy copy
- ID proof

For Vehicle Insurance:
- FIR (if serious)
- Photos of the damage
- Repair bills
- Driving license and registration

For Life Insurance:
- Death certificate
- Policy document
- ID and bank details of the nominee

What Is Cashless vs. Reimbursement?

Kabir asked, "What's the deal with cashless treatment?"

"In a cashless claim" said Zara, "the insurance company pays the hospital directly. You don't have to pay upfront".

"But it only works in network hospitals" added Ananya.

"If the hospital isn't part of the network" said Rohan, "**you pay first and then file for reimbursement**".

Common Reasons Claims Get Rejected

Aarav listed a few:
- Not disclosing a **pre-existing illness**
- Claiming during the **waiting period**
- Not following proper **procedure**
- Submitting wrong or **incomplete documents**

"People often get angry at the insurer" said Ananya. "But many rejections happen because of mistakes made by the policyholder".

"That's why reading the terms and conditions matters" said Zara.

Case Studies: The Good and the Bad

Rohan shared two short examples:

Good: Aman had a motor accident. He clicked photos, informed the insurer within 2 hours, submitted all papers, and got his car repaired through a network garage. The process was smooth.

Not So Good: Maya bought health insurance but didn't tell them about her diabetes. She was hospitalised six months later, and her claim was rejected because of nondisclosure.

"Lesson?" asked Ananya. "Always be honest and prompt".

Grievance Redressal

"What if the company still rejects the claim unfairly?" Kabir asked.

"You can file a complaint with **IRDAI through the Integrated Grievance Management System (IGMS)**" said Zara.

"And if needed, escalate it to the **Insurance Ombudsman**" added Rohan.

"There are channels to help if you feel cheated" said Ananya.

Quick Recap

Zara wrapped up:
- A claim is your way of using your insurance when something goes wrong
- Inform early, submit documents, and follow the steps
- Understand cashless and reimbursement options
- Claims get rejected often due to incorrect info or missing documents
- Help is available through IRDAI and the Ombudsman if needed

"Next up" said Ananya, "we ask the big question - who actually needs insurance and when?"

The Piggy Bank Society walked out, a little more cautious but also more prepared. Insurance wasn't just about buying. It was about knowing what to do when you really needed it.

Chapter 7

Should Everyone Buy Insurance?

The next meeting of the Piggy Bank Society began with a fun debate. Zara wrote a question on the board: *"Is insurance necessary for everyone?"*

Kabir raised his hand quickly. "Only rich people need insurance. They have more to lose".

"But poor people can't afford to lose anything" countered Ananya. "So maybe they need it more".

Rohan nodded. "Let's break it down. Who needs insurance, when, and what kind?"

Life Stages and Insurance Needs

Zara sketched a timeline on the board:

1. Children and Teenagers
- Usually don't need life insurance
- But might be covered under family health plans

Insurance may not feel urgent until something unexpected happens. It's a choice between hoping for luck… or choosing preparation

2. Young Adults
- Starting to earn money
- Should get term insurance and health insurance

3. Married with Dependents
- Need life insurance to protect the family's future
- Health insurance becomes even more important

4. Older Adults / Retirees
- Focus on health insurance
- Life insurance may not be needed if there are no financial dependents

Choosing the Right Type of Insurance

"Don't just buy everything" said Ananya. "Pick insurance based on what risks you actually face".

Rohan explained:
- If you ride a bike: get motor insurance
- If you're the only earning member: term life insurance
- If your parents are aging: health insurance for senior citizens
- If you run a business: property or liability insurance

"Insurance is not about fear" added Zara. *"It's about responsibility"*.

How Much Insurance Do You Need?

Kabir asked, "What if I take a ₹50 lakh life cover? Is that enough?"

"It depends" said Rohan. "How much money would your family need if you weren't around?"

Ananya broke it down:
- Cover your loans (like home or car loans)
- Future education expenses for kids
- Daily expenses for 10–15 years

"Same with health insurance" said Aarav. "Check hospital costs in your city and choose accordingly".

What About the Cost?

"Premiums can be expensive" said Kabir. "How do people afford it?"

"Start with what you can manage" said Ananya. "Even a basic plan is better than nothing".

"There are also government schemes" said Zara.

Rohan listed a few:

- **PMJJBY** – Life insurance for ₹2 lakh, premium ₹436 per year

- **PMSBY** – Accident cover for ₹2 lakh, premium ₹20 per year
- **Ayushman Bharat** – Health cover for low-income families

"These plans are simple, affordable, and good for first-time users" said Aarav.

Underinsurance and Overinsurance

"Some people buy too little insurance" said Ananya. "That's called *underinsurance*".

"And some buy way more than they need" said Rohan. "That's *overinsurance*".

Zara said, "Both are risky. One leaves you unprotected. The other wastes money"

When Insurance Isn't the Answer

"Insurance helps manage financial risk, not every kind of problem" said Ananya.
"It won't stop things from going wrong" said Kabir.

"But it will help you bounce back faster" said Rohan.

"And that makes all the difference" said Zara.

Quick Recap

Aarav summarised:

- Not everyone needs the same type of insurance
- Choose based on age, responsibilities, and lifestyle
- Buy enough coverage to meet real needs, not guesses
- Use government schemes if budgets are tight
- Avoid overinsuring or ignoring real risks

"Next up" said Ananya, "we'll peek into the future of insurance - apps, AI, and how insurance is becoming smarter every day".

The Piggy Bank Society left with a question buzzing in their heads: If something went wrong tomorrow, would they or their families be ready?

Chapter 8

The Insurance of Tomorrow

It was the last session of the term and the Piggy Bank Society had decided to meet in their favourite spot by the window. The weather was calm, but the conversation was buzzing.

"Do you think insurance will still be around when we grow up?" asked Kabir.

"Definitely" said Zara. "But it might look very different. That's what today's chapter is about - the future of insurance".

Going Digital

Rohan held up his phone. "People already buy insurance online. No more filling long forms with a pen".

Ananya added, "Now, there are apps where you can buy, renew, and track policies. Some even let you file claims in a few taps".

As the world changes, so do the risks. Insurance of tomorrow must protect us in ways we're only beginning to imagine today

"It's called **digital insurance,** and it's growing fast" said Aarav.

"And it's making insurance simpler and more accessible" said Zara.

What Is InsurTech?

Kabir asked, "Is there a word for all this tech-insurance stuff?"

"Yes" said Rohan. "It's called **InsurTech - a mix of Insurance and Technology**".

Ananya explained, "These companies use technology to:

- Sell insurance instantly
- Use AI to approve claims faster
- Offer personalised plans
- Chat with customers through bots"

"And it's not just private companies" said Aarav. "Even IRDAI is pushing for faster, smarter systems".

Microinsurance and Inclusion

Zara shared an example. "In some parts of India, *you can buy insurance for just ₹10 a month*".

"That's microinsurance" said Ananya. "Tiny premiums, but enough to cover basic needs".

"It's made for people who don't earn much but still face risks" added Rohan.

"And it helps bring more people into the safety net" said Aarav.

Smart Devices and Instant Alerts

"Imagine your smartwatch sending data to your insurer" said Zara. "If your heart rate goes high, it notifies your doctor too".

"Or your car sends an accident alert, and insurance starts the claim automatically" said Rohan.

"That's the power of *connected devices*" said Ananya. "They could make claims faster and safer".

AI and Fraud Detection

"Insurance companies are also using Artificial Intelligence" said Aarav.

"To detect fake claims, spot patterns, and even suggest better plans" said Zara.

Rohan added, "Some companies use chatbots that answer your questions 24x7, without needing a human".

"But people still want real advice for big things" said Ananya. "So tech supports humans, not replaces them".

Green Insurance and Climate Risks

"What about the environment?" asked Kabir.

"There's a new idea called green insurance" said Ananya. "It covers *solar panels, electric cars, and even protects businesses against climate events*".

"As the world changes, insurance must change too" said Zara.

Learning to Be Ready

"Whatever shape insurance takes" said Rohan, "being informed will always help".

Ananya listed future-ready tips:
- Understand your own risks
- Choose smart, digital options
- Use only trusted sources
- Don't ignore fine print - even online

"Technology makes it easy" said Aarav, "but the responsibility is still ours".

Quick Recap

Before they packed up, Zara summarised:

- Insurance is going digital with apps, AI, and connected devices
- Microinsurance is making it accessible for all
- InsurTech is helping speed up processes
- Green and personalised insurance are on the rise
- Staying informed is the smartest policy of all

"As insurance evolves" said Ananya, "so should we".

"Because the future doesn't wait" said Rohan.

"And being prepared" said Zara, "never goes out of style".

The Piggy Bank Society closed their notebooks and shared a quiet smile. They had explored risks, responsibility, and readiness. And that was a great way to end the chapter - not just in the book, but in life too.

DECODING STOCK MARKETS

Chapter 1

What Is the Stock Market, Really?

It was a bright Tuesday afternoon, and the Piggy Bank Society had just finished their midterm exams. The school library felt like a perfect retreat. As they gathered around their usual corner, Ananya pulled out a board game box with the words **"Stock Market Simulator"** written on it.

Kabir looked curious. "Is this like Monopoly?"

"Kind of" said Ananya. "But this time, we're not just buying properties. We're buying pieces of real companies".

Zara tilted her head. "Wait, real companies? Like the ones that make our chocolates or phones?"

"Exactly" said Rohan. "Welcome to the world of the stock market".

The stock market is like a big marketplace where people buy tiny pieces of companies, hoping their value will grow over time

The Marketplace of Companies

Ananya wrote on the whiteboard:

Stock Market = A place where people buy and sell shares of companies.

"Think of it like a giant bazaar" she said. "But instead of vegetables or clothes, what's being bought and sold are little pieces of companies".

Kabir raised his hand. "Why would companies sell pieces of themselves?"

"Good question" said Aarav. "When companies want to grow, they need money. They can borrow it from banks or raise it from people like us. That's where the stock market comes in".

"So when I buy a share, I'm giving money to the company to grow?" asked Zara.

"Exactly" said Rohan. "In return, you own a tiny part of that company".

Why Do People Invest in Stocks?

Zara added, "If the company does well, your share becomes more valuable. You can sell it later for a higher price".

"Or sometimes you get a dividend" said Ananya. "That's like a small reward or profit share from the company".

Kabir looked impressed. "So instead of just saving, people invest to grow their money?"

"Yes" said Rohan. "But investing comes with risks too. The company might not do well, and your share could lose value".

Not a Physical Market

Aarav asked, "So where is the stock market? Like a big building?"

"In the old days, yes" said Ananya. "Now most of it happens digitally through **stock exchanges like NSE and BSE**".

Kabir smiled. "So, I could technically own a piece of a company from my phone?"

"Totally" said Zara. "That's what makes it exciting and powerful. But you need to know how it works before jumping in".

Real-Life Connection

Rohan pulled out a newspaper. "See this? It's the business section. These numbers show how different company stocks are doing".

"Like a scoreboard for businesses" said Kabir.

"Exactly" said Ananya. "But behind those numbers are real people making decisions, buying, selling, investing and reacting to news".

Quick Recap

Ananya summarised:
- The stock market is where people buy and sell parts of companies
- Companies raise money by selling shares
- Investors buy shares hoping their value will grow
- It mostly happens online on exchanges like NSE and BSE

The Piggy Bank Society looked at the board game again, this time with a lot more curiosity. The stock market wasn't just for adults in suits. It was something they could understand, explore, and maybe even be part of.

Chapter 2

Stocks and Shares - Owning a Piece of a Company

The next day, the Piggy Bank Society met with even more excitement. Ananya had brought along a chocolate bar, a pair of scissors, and a big smile.

"Who wants some chocolate?" she asked.

Five hands shot up instantly.

She unwrapped the bar and started cutting it into small pieces.

"Each of you gets a piece. Now imagine this chocolate bar is a company. When I gave you a piece, I gave you part ownership".

Kabir grinned. "So I own a piece of 'Choco Corp'?"

"Exactly" said Ananya. "That's what a share is".

When you buy a stock, you're buying a piece of a company. That means you share in its wins, and learn from its losses

What Is a Share?

Zara wrote on the board:

Share = A piece of ownership in a company.

"When a company wants to grow, it sells shares. People who buy those shares become partial owners" she explained.

Rohan added, "If a company has 1,000 shares and you buy 10, you own 1 percent of it".

"Even if it's a tiny slice, it still counts" said Aarav.

Owning Means Believing

Ananya said, "People buy shares because they believe in the company's future".

"If the company does well, the share price usually goes up. If it struggles, the price can fall" explained Rohan.

Kabir asked, "But do I get to make decisions if I own a share?"

"Not really" said Zara. "You're an owner, but decisions are made by a board of directors. You can vote in some big meetings if you own enough shares, though".

Real-Life Example

Aarav said, "Let's say there's a sneaker company called SwiftStep. You love their shoes and think they'll grow bigger. If you buy shares in SwiftStep, you're betting they'll succeed".

"And if they open more stores and earn more profits, your share value may rise" said Rohan.

"Or you might get a dividend which is a reward paid to shareholders when the company makes a profit" added Ananya.

IPO: The First Time Shares Go Public

Zara explained, "When a private company decides to sell shares to the public for the first time, it launches an **IPO — Initial Public Offering**".

"It's like a company saying, 'Hey world, want to own a piece of us?'" said Kabir.

"After the IPO, those shares can be bought and sold in the stock market" said Rohan.

Price Changes and Ownership

Ananya added, "Even if the price of a share goes up or down every day, the number of shares you own stays the same".

"So my chocolate piece is still mine, even if its value changes?" asked Kabir.

"Exactly" said Zara. "But you can choose to sell it when you think the time is right".

Quick Recap

Rohan summarised:

- A share is a small piece of a company
- Buying a share means you're a partial owner
- Shares can go up or down in value based on company performance
- IPOs are how companies offer shares to the public for the first time
- You can earn profits through rising share prices or dividends

The Piggy Bank Society members looked at their tiny chocolate pieces with pride. They weren't just treats now - they were metaphors for ownership, risk, and opportunity.

Chapter 3

The Players in the Game

The Piggy Bank Society gathered around the whiteboard as Ananya drew a big circle in the center and labeled it **"Stock Market"**. Then she started drawing arrows pointing toward it from all sides.

"Today" she said, "we're meeting the people and groups that make the stock market what it is".

Kabir leaned in. "So, who are we playing with?"

Zara grinned. "More like, who's already playing".

The Retail Investor

Rohan began, *"This is you, me, our parents and all the everyday people who buy small amounts of shares"*.

"They're called retail investors" said Ananya. "They usually invest through apps or brokers".

The stock market works because many players each do their part - from investing and managing, to keeping it all fair and smooth

Kabir added, "So when my dad checks stock prices on his phone, that's him being a retail investor?"

"Exactly" said Zara.

The Big Institutions

Aarav pointed to another arrow labeled **"Institutional Investors"**.

"These are big players" he explained. "Like *mutual fund houses, insurance companies, pension funds*. They invest huge amounts of money".

"They often buy lakhs or crores worth of shares at a time" said Rohan.

"Because they manage money for a lot of people" added Ananya.

Traders vs. Investors

Zara said, "Not everyone in the market plays the long game".

"Some people are traders" explained Rohan. *"They buy and sell shares quickly to make a profit from small price changes"*.

"While investors usually hold on for longer even sometimes years" added Aarav.

Kabir nodded. "So traders are like sprinters, and investors are marathon runners".

"Well said" smiled Ananya.

Stock Brokers

"Brokers help people buy and sell shares" said Zara. *"They act as the middle person between you and the stock exchange"*.

"Some popular brokers in India are Zerodha, Upstox, Groww" said Rohan.

"You open a demat account through them, place your order, and they handle the rest" said Ananya.

Regulators: The Rule Makers

Aarav wrote one word in bold: **SEBI**

"SEBI stands for *Securities and Exchange Board of India*" he said. "It's the government body that regulates the stock market".

"They make sure everyone plays fair" said Zara.

"If someone cheats or manipulates prices, SEBI steps in" added Rohan.

"It's like the referee of the stock market" said Kabir.

Media and Analysts

"News channels, websites, YouTubers : they all talk about the market" said Ananya.

"Some share tips, others analyse company performance" said Zara.

"Just remember" added Rohan, "**not all advice is good advice. Always do your own research**".

Quick Recap

Aarav summarised:
- Retail investors are everyday people like us
- Institutional investors are big money players
- Traders buy and sell quickly, investors hold for the long term
- Brokers help us place orders in the market
- SEBI is the rule-maker and protector of fairness
- Media and analysts give info, but you should think for yourself

"Next time" said Ananya, "we'll explore where the magic happens - the stock exchanges of India".

The Piggy Bank Society left feeling like they had just walked into a giant stadium. The game was on, and now they knew who was on the field.

Chapter 4

Stock Exchanges in India

The next Piggy Bank Society meeting began with Rohan bringing two cardboard cutouts labeled **BSE** and **NSE**.

"These are not just letters" he said. "They are where the stock market comes alive in India".

Kabir leaned forward. "So these are like the stores where you buy the shares?"

"Kind of" said Ananya. "Let's explore how they work".

What Is a Stock Exchange?

Zara wrote on the board:

Stock Exchange = A platform where buyers and sellers trade shares.

"In India, we mainly have two big stock exchanges - *the Bombay Stock Exchange (BSE) and the National Stock Exchange (NSE)*" said Ananya.

Stock exchanges like the BSE and NSE are where shares are bought and sold every day like a busy market for companies!

BSE: Asia's Oldest

Rohan said, "BSE was founded in 1875. That's even older than most of our grandparents".

"It's located in Mumbai, and one of its major indicators is the Sensex" said Zara.

"Sensex tracks the performance of 30 major companies listed on BSE" explained Ananya.

"So if Sensex is up, it means these top companies are doing well?" asked Kabir.

"Generally, yes" said Aarav.

NSE: India's Giant

"NSE was started in 1992 and brought in more digital systems" said Rohan.

"Its index is called the **Nifty 50 and it shows how 50 top companies are performing**" said Zara.

"It's fast, modern, and handles a huge number of trades daily" added Ananya.

How Trading Happens

Aarav explained, "Let's say you want to buy one share of a company listed on NSE".

"You place an order through your broker. It gets matched with someone selling that share. The trade is completed electronically" said Rohan.

"This process is called **T+1 settlement - trade plus one day to complete it**" said Zara.

"That means if you buy today, the share is credited to your account by tomorrow" said Ananya.

Listing a Company

Kabir asked, "How does a company get its shares on NSE or BSE?"

"They have to go through a listing process" said Rohan. *"They file details with SEBI, go public through an IPO, and get approval from the exchange"*.

"Only then can their shares be traded" said Aarav.

Trading Hours

Zara said, "Stock markets in India open at **9:15 AM and close at 3:30 PM, Monday to Friday**".

"Outside of that, there's no trading" said Ananya.

"So it's like school hours, but for money" joked Kabir.

Everyone laughed.

Quick Recap

Ananya summed up:

- Stock exchanges are platforms where shares are bought and sold
- BSE and NSE are India's two main exchanges
- Sensex and Nifty 50 track how top companies are doing
- Trading is done electronically and settles in one day
- Companies must get listed to be traded
- Trading happens during fixed hours on weekdays

"Next time" said Zara, "we'll talk about bulls, bears, and why the market sometimes feels like a roller coaster".

The Piggy Bank Society felt like they had just toured the engine room of the Indian financial system. The more they learned, the more real the market felt.

Chapter 5

Bulls, Bears, and Market Mood Swings

The next day, when the Piggy Bank Society walked into the library, they found two stuffed animals on the table - **a bull and a bear.**

Kabir laughed, "Are we doing a wildlife class today?"

Ananya shook her head. "These two animals represent the moods of the stock market".

Rohan added, "The market moves up and down all the time. And how people feel plays a big part".

Bull Market: The Optimistic Climb

Zara wrote on the board:

Bull Market = When stock prices are rising and investors feel confident.

Markets go up like bulls and down like bears, driven by emotions, news, and expectations. That's why it's called a mood swing!

"Imagine a bull charging ahead, horns pointed upward" said Rohan. "That's why it's used to show a rising market".

"In a bull market, people are buying more shares, expecting prices to go higher" explained Aarav.

"Investors feel hopeful, companies are growing, and everyone wants in" said Ananya.

Bear Market: The Careful Retreat

"Now the bear" said Zara. *"It swipes its paws downward. That's why a falling market is called a bear market"*.

Bear Market = When stock prices are falling and investors are nervous.

"In a bear market, people are afraid. They sell shares, which pushes prices down even more" said Rohan.

"Everyone becomes cautious. It's like holding on to your money and waiting for things to settle" said Ananya.

What Causes These Swings?

Aarav explained, "The stock market reacts to news, emotions, and world events".

"Good news like higher profits or new inventions can make markets rise" said Zara.

"Bad news like wars, inflation, or job losses can make them fall" added Rohan.

"A mix of facts and feelings" said Ananya.

Investor Psychology

Kabir asked, "So people panic when others panic?"

"Yes" said Rohan. "That's called **herd behavior.** If everyone is buying, you feel like buying too. If they're selling, you want to sell".

"But smart investors stay calm. They look at the long term" said Zara.

"Just like not judging a movie by its first five minutes" said Ananya.

Volatility: The Market's Mood Swings

Zara wrote another word:

Volatility = How much the market moves up and down in a short time.

"If prices keep jumping around, the market is said to be volatile" said Aarav.

"It can happen during elections, budget announcements, or global events" added Rohan.

Handling the Swings

"Don't let emotions control your actions" said Ananya.

"Have a plan, and stick to it" said Zara. "If your goal is long term, don't worry about small dips".

Kabir nodded, "Like riding a roller coaster. You hold tight and wait for it to pass".

"Exactly" said Rohan. *"And sometimes, the best thing to do is nothing"*.

Quick Recap

Ananya summarised:

- Bull market means prices are rising and people are confident
- Bear market means prices are falling and people are cautious
- Emotions, news, and global events move the market
- Volatility means frequent ups and downs
- Stay calm and focus on long-term goals

"Next time" said Zara, "we'll learn how to actually buy and sell shares. Because theory is great, but action makes it real".

The Piggy Bank Society left with a better understanding of the market's emotions. It was not just about numbers - it was about people too.

Chapter 6

How Do You
Buy or Sell a Stock?

The Piggy Bank Society walked into the library to find a giant flowchart stuck on the wall. At the top, it said, **"How to Buy a Stock in India"**.

Ananya clapped her hands. "Time to go from theory to action".

Kabir smiled. "Let me guess. It's not like going to a grocery shop, right?"

"Not quite" said Zara. "But it's also not rocket science".

Step 1: Open a Demat Account

Rohan started, "First, you need a Demat account. That's where your shares are stored digitally like a digital locker".

"You also need a trading account to place buy and sell orders" added Ananya.

Buying or selling a stock is easier than you think, when you know the steps and understand the responsibility

"These are usually provided by brokers like Zerodha, Groww, Upstox, or banks" said Aarav.

Step 2: Fund Your Account

"Once your accounts are set up, you transfer money into them" said Zara. "That's your buying power".

Kabir asked, "So I can't just click and buy without money in it?"

"Exactly" said Rohan. "The money has to be there first".

Step 3: Choose the Stock

"Now comes the exciting part" said Ananya. "Decide which company's shares you want to buy".

"You can search by the company's name or ticker symbol" said Zara. "Like TCS, HDFC, or Infosys".

"Make sure you've done your research" added Aarav. "Don't just follow trends".

Step 4: Place the Order

Rohan explained, "You can place a market order or a limit order".

- **Market order:** Buy at the current market price
- **Limit order:** Buy only if the price falls to a certain level you choose

"You can also choose how many shares you want to buy" said Ananya.

Step 5: Trade Execution

"Once you place the order, it goes to the stock exchange through your broker" said Zara.

"If someone is selling that stock at your price, the trade happens instantly" said Rohan.

"This is all digital. You get confirmation on your app or email" said Ananya.

Step 6: T+1 Settlement

Aarav said, "T+1 means the transaction is settled one working day after the trade".

"If you buy today, the shares show up in your demat account by tomorrow" said Zara.

"And if you sell, you get the money the next day too" added Rohan.

Step 7: Track or Sell

Kabir asked, "What happens after I buy?"

"You can track the investment and watch how the share performs" said Ananya.

"When you feel it's the right time, you can sell it using the same process in reverse" said Aarav.

Quick Recap

Zara summarised:

- Open a demat and trading account
- Fund your account with money
- Pick a stock after research
- Place a market or limit order
- Let the broker and exchange handle the trade
- Shares are delivered by the next day (T+1)
- You can track or sell anytime

The Piggy Bank Society now knew how to buy a stock. What was once a mystery was now just a series of steps they could follow.

Chapter 7

Risks, Rewards, and Why Prices Fluctuate

The library was quieter than usual when the Piggy Bank Society gathered for their next session. On the table were two balloons : *one rising and one deflating.*

"Today" said Ananya, "we're talking about why stock prices rise and fall. It's not magic. It's a mix of logic, emotion, and news".

What Moves Stock Prices?

Rohan wrote on the board:

Stock Price = What buyers are willing to pay and sellers are willing to accept.

"It's all about demand and supply" said Zara. "If more people want to buy a stock, the price goes up. If more people want to sell, the price goes down".

Stock prices change for many reasons - profits, news, emotions, and even chance. Learning to understand them helps you invest smarter

Kabir nodded. "So it's like cricket tickets. If everyone wants one, the price shoots up".

"Exactly" said Ananya.

Company Performance

Aarav added, "If a company is doing well by making profits, launching new products, people want to buy its shares".

"That's why quarterly results matter. If earnings are strong, prices often go up" said Rohan.

"And if there's bad news like losses or layoffs, prices can fall" said Zara.

News and Announcements

Ananya said, "Stock prices react quickly to news both good or bad".

"Government budgets, RBI decisions, international events, even tweets from CEOs can shake the market" said Rohan.

Kabir laughed. "A single tweet can move millions?"

"Yes" said Zara. "Markets are emotional".

Investor Sentiment

"Sometimes, prices go up just because everyone feels positive, even if nothing has changed" said Aarav.

"That's called **market sentiment**" said Ananya. *"It's like the mood of investors"*.

"But moods can change fast" added Rohan.

Rumours and Speculation

Zara warned, "Not all price moves are based on facts. Sometimes people follow rumours".

"Speculation is when people guess what might happen and trade based on that" said Aarav.

"That's risky" said Ananya. "Because guesses are not always right".

Understanding Risk

Kabir asked, "So what makes investing risky?"

"Prices can drop suddenly" said Zara. "Even good companies can face setbacks".

Rohan said, "That's why you don't put all your money into one stock".

"Diversify. Spread your risk" said Ananya.

Rewards of Investing

"But with risk comes reward" said Aarav. "If you pick the right stock and hold it long enough, your money can grow a lot".

"Some stocks have doubled or tripled over years" said Rohan.

"Long-term investors usually win the game" said Zara.

Quick Recap

Ananya closed the session:
- Stock prices change on demand and supply
- Company results, news, and public mood play a big role
- Rumours and guesses can be risky
- Diversify to manage risk
- Long-term investing brings rewards

The Piggy Bank Society left with a better understanding of those dancing numbers on the screen. Behind every price, there was a story.

Chapter 8

Can Kids Be Investors Too?

The final session of the Piggy Bank Society's stock market adventure began with a big question written on the board:
Can kids be investors too?

Kabir read it aloud. "Is this a trick question?"

"Not at all" said Ananya. "You might not be able to open a stock account by yourself yet, but that doesn't mean you can't learn how investing works".

Learning Before Earning

Zara said, "Most adults invest without really understanding what they're doing.

You don't need real money to start learning. With curiosity, kids can build the habits of smart investors today for a brighter tomorrow

But we're getting a head start".

"Investing is more than buying shares. It's about developing good habits" added Rohan.

"Like thinking long-term, being patient, and doing your own research" said Aarav.

Virtual Stock Market Games

Ananya shared, "There are apps and websites that simulate the stock market. You get fake money and real-time data to practice investing".

"It's like a video game but with financial skills" said Kabir.

"Games like these teach you how the market moves without using real money" said Zara.

Investing with Parents

Rohan said, "You can also ask your parents to open a **minor demat account.** They manage it, but you can help pick the stocks".

"It becomes a family activity" said Aarav. "You learn by watching and asking questions".

"You can also track a few companies you love : like a favourite food or tech brand and follow their stock price" said Ananya.

Start with Mutual Funds

Kabir asked, "Is there a safer way to begin?"

"Yes" said Zara. "Mutual funds are a good option. We'll cover them in a future conversation, but just know they let you invest in many stocks at once".

"Less risk, more learning" added Rohan.

Key Tips for Young Investors

Ananya listed out a few golden rules:

- Learn before you leap
- Avoid shortcuts or hot tips
- Stay calm during ups and downs
- Ask questions and seek advice
- Focus on long-term goals

"You don't need a lot of money to start. You need curiosity" said Zara.

The Final Recap

Rohan summarised the journey:

- The stock market is where shares of companies are bought and sold
- Shares give you partial ownership in a company
- Prices move based on performance, news, and emotions
- You can buy stocks using demat and trading accounts
- Risk is real, but rewards grow over time
- Even kids can learn, track, and invest with support

"In a future meeting" said Ananya, "we dive into mutual funds the way to invest without picking each stock yourself".

The Piggy Bank Society had come a long way. They didn't just understand the stock market now but they respected it. And as they walked out of the library, each of them felt like a future investor already taking shape.

MUTUAL FUNDS MADE EASY

Chapter 1

What on Earth is a Mutual Fund?

It was a rainy Friday afternoon, and the Piggy Bank Society had taken shelter in the library, their cozy hideout for money adventures. Ananya walked in carrying a giant tiffin box.

"Group lunch?" asked Kabir hopefully.

"Sort of" said Ananya, placing it on the table. "Today, we're going to talk about **mutual funds**. And this tiffin is going to help us understand".

The others leaned in, intrigued.

The Group Lunch Analogy

Ananya opened the tiffin to reveal four compartments: rice, dal, sabzi, and sweets. She also handed out four small plates to Kabir, Zara, Aarav, and Rohan.

A mutual fund is like a team fund - everyone contributes, and a fund manager decides how to use it best. When we invest together, we can afford more and share the rewards

"Imagine each of us brought ₹50 to contribute to this lunch" she began. "Together, we pooled ₹200. I went out and bought this combo tiffin for all of us".

"So instead of each of us buying separate meals, we joined our money and got a full meal together" said Zara.

"Exactly" said Ananya. "That's the idea behind a mutual fund".

The Basic Idea

Rohan wrote on the board:

Mutual Fund = A pool of money collected from many people, invested in different things by an expert.

"It's like a team investment" explained Aarav. "You don't need to know everything about where to put your money. You trust the expert - *the fund manager* - to do it for you".

Kabir nodded slowly. "So instead of buying a single stock myself, I put my money into a mutual fund and it gets invested in many stocks or bonds?"

"Bingo" said Zara.

Why Do People Choose Mutual Funds?

Ananya listed a few reasons:

- *You don't need a lot of money to start*
- *Your money gets spread across different investments*
- *A professional manages your investment*
- *You can invest little by little (like monthly SIPs)*

"It's great for people who don't have time to study the stock market but still want to grow their money" she added.

Real-Life Example

Zara said, "My uncle started a Systematic Investment Plan (SIP) for ₹500 a month when I was born. Now it's worth more than ₹1 lakh".

"See?" said Rohan. "That's the power of starting early and staying consistent".

"It's like planting a money plant" said Kabir. "Water it regularly, and it grows".

Quick Recap

Aarav summarised:

- A mutual fund pools money from many investors
- A fund manager decides where to invest that money
- It helps people invest in a variety of things without needing to be experts
- Even small amounts, invested regularly, can grow big over time

"Next time" said Ananya, "we'll open the box further and see how mutual funds actually work - from SIPs to fund managers".

The Piggy Bank Society packed up, but Kabir couldn't stop thinking about the lunch analogy. If money could be mixed, managed, and made to grow like a good tiffin, he was definitely hungry to learn more.

Chapter 2

How Do Mutual Funds Work?

The next time the Piggy Bank Society met in the library, Ananya brought a small whiteboard and drew a large jar labeled "Mutual Fund." She then drew stick figures around it, each dropping coins into the jar.

"This is how mutual funds begin" she said. "Lots of people, each putting in a little money".

Kabir looked thoughtful. "But who decides what to do with all that money?"

"That's where the *fund manager* comes in" said Zara. "Think of them as the captain of the ship".

The Role of the Fund Manager

Rohan wrote on the board:

Fund Manager = The expert who decides where to invest the pooled money.

A fund manager identifies the right mix of investments to make sure that the fund aims to consistently beat the benchmark

"They study the market, pick stocks or bonds, and manage the fund to try and get good returns" said Aarav.

"So I don't choose the companies myself?" asked Kabir.

"Nope" said Ananya. "You trust the fund manager to choose a mix of investments based on the fund's goal".

SIP: Small Steps to Big Goals

Zara said, "One of the coolest parts of mutual funds is the **SIP - Systematic Investment Plan**".

"You can invest a fixed amount every month, like ₹500 or ₹1,000" said Rohan.

"It's like setting a reminder to invest regularly" said Ananya. "And over time, your money grows with consistency".

"It's like a money gym membership" said Kabir. "Keep showing up, and the results come".

Where Does the Money Go?

Aarav explained, "It depends on the type of mutual fund. It could go into:

- *Company shares (equity)*
- *Government bonds (debt)*
- *A mix of both (hybrid)"*

"Different funds have different goals. Some are for growth, some are for safety, and some for a mix" said Zara.

The Mutual Fund Fact Sheet

Ananya pulled out a printout. "This is called a **factsheet**. It shows:

- *Where the money is invested*
- *Past performance*
- *Risk level*
- *Who manages the fund"*

Kabir scanned it. "It's like a report card for the mutual fund".

"Exactly" said Rohan. "And it helps you decide if the fund matches your goal".

Quick Recap

Zara summarised:

- A fund manager makes the investment decisions
- SIP helps you invest regularly in small amounts
- Funds can invest in equity, debt, or both
- Factsheets give you the full picture of the fund's activity

"Next time" said Ananya, "we'll explore the different types of mutual funds. Because not all funds are the same - each one has its own personality".

The Piggy Bank Society packed their bags, feeling like they had just stepped into the control room of their own financial spaceship. And now they knew who was piloting it.

Chapter 3

Types of Mutual Funds

It was a bright Saturday morning, and the Piggy Bank Society had gathered early for a special session. Ananya walked in with three color-coded folders - red, green, and yellow.

"These are not just folders" she said. "They represent the three main types of mutual funds. Let's decode them together".

Kabir leaned forward. "Let me guess - red is risky?"

"Spot on" said Zara. "And that's just the beginning".

Equity Funds: High Risk, High Reward

Ananya held up the red folder.

Mutual funds come in different types - some aim to grow fast, others stay steady. Knowing what each one offers helps you pick the fund that's right for you

Equity Funds = Invest mainly in company shares.

"These are like roller coasters" said Rohan. "They go up and down based on how the stock market performs".

"They can give great returns over time, but they're not ideal if you need the money in a few months" added Zara.

"Good for *long-term goals* like college savings or starting a business one day" said Aarav.

Debt Funds: Low Risk, Steady Returns

Next, Ananya picked up the green folder.

Debt Funds = Invest in government bonds, company loans, and fixed-income securities.

"These are like slow and steady turtles" said Kabir. "They don't move fast, but they're reliable".

"People use them when they want safety and regular income" said Ananya.

"Perfect for *short-term goals* or for someone who can't handle big swings" added Rohan.

Hybrid Funds: The Best of Both Worlds

Finally, Ananya held up the yellow folder.

Hybrid Funds = Mix of equity and debt.

"Balanced + flexible" said Zara. "They give you a taste of both growth + safety"

"Think of it as a thali - you get a little bit of everything" said Aarav.

"Great for beginners who want to try investing without jumping fully into the stock market" added Ananya.

Choosing the Right Fund

Rohan said, "The right fund depends on three things:
1. **Your goal**
2. **Your time horizon**
3. **Your risk comfort"**

"If you need the money soon, debt might be better. If you're saving for something far away, equity can help you grow faster" said Zara.

"And if you're unsure, hybrid is a safe start" said Kabir.

Quick Recap

Ananya summarised:

- Equity funds offer high returns but come with more risk
- Debt funds are safer and more stable
- Hybrid funds offer a balanced mix
- Your fund choice should match your goal, time, and risk comfort

"Next time" said Rohan, "we'll learn how to check if a mutual fund is doing well. Because choosing the fund is just the beginning".

The Piggy Bank Society left the room feeling like fund detectives, ready to match every financial goal with the right mutual fund partner.

Chapter 4

NAV, Returns, and What to Track

The library table was covered in colorful charts and graphs when the Piggy Bank Society arrived. Ananya pointed to one that showed wavy lines going up and down.

"Today, we talk about how to track your mutual funds - and understand what these squiggly lines mean".

Kabir squinted. "Looks like a snake doing yoga".

Zara laughed. "That's your mutual fund's performance over time".

What is NAV?

Rohan wrote on the board:

NAV = Net Asset Value. It tells you the price of one unit of a mutual fund.

Tracking your investment is like monitoring a plant's growth. NAV tells you how much it's worth today, but long-term returns show how healthy it's been over time

"It's like the MRP of a chocolate bar" explained Ananya. "But instead of cocoa, this one contains stocks or bonds".

"If you invest ₹1,000 and the NAV is ₹100, you get 10 units of that fund" said Zara.

"And the NAV changes daily based on how the investments inside the fund perform" said Aarav.

How Returns Are Calculated

Kabir asked, "How do we know if our fund is doing well?"

Ananya said, *"You compare today's NAV with the NAV from when you invested"*.

"If NAV goes up, your investment grows. If it drops, you've lost a bit - on paper" said Rohan.

Zara added, "Always look at longer time frames like 1 year, 3 years, or 5 years to see the real picture".

Key Things to Track

Aarav made a list:

- **Returns** – *How much your investment has grown over time*
- **Expense Ratio** – *The fee the fund charges to manage your money*
- **Fund Manager** – *The person making the investment decisions*
- **Portfolio** – *Where the money is invested (stocks, bonds, sectors)*

"If the expense ratio is too high, it eats into your returns" said Ananya.

"And if the fund keeps changing its investments too often, it might be too risky" said Rohan.

Comparing with Benchmarks

Zara said, *"Funds are often compared with benchmarks like Nifty or Sensex"*.

"If your fund performs better than its benchmark, that's a good sign" said Aarav.

"But don't expect it to always beat the market" said Ananya. "Consistency matters more".

Where to Track This Info

Kabir asked, "Where can I see all this stuff?"

Rohan replied, *"Most mutual fund apps, websites, or even newspapers show this data. Look for a fund factsheet or monthly report"*.

Zara added, "Even kids can track this with the help of parents. It's like checking your scoreboard".

Quick Recap

Ananya summarised:

- NAV is the price of one unit of a mutual fund
- Returns show how much your investment has grown
- Expense ratio, fund manager, and portfolio matter
- Compare with benchmarks to judge performance
- Use apps or factsheets to track progress

The Piggy Bank Society packed their bags, already planning to check the NAV of a fund before dinner. Money, after all, was starting to feel like a game they could win by playing smart.

Chapter 5

How to Start Investing in Mutual Funds

The Piggy Bank Society met on a sunny Wednesday afternoon. Ananya walked in holding a smartphone and a small notepad.

"Today" she said, "we're going to talk about how to actually start investing in mutual funds".

Kabir raised his hand. "Wait, do I need a bank account or something?"

"Yes, and a few other things" said Zara. "Let's break it down".

Step 1: KYC - Know Your Customer

Rohan wrote on the board:

KYC = A basic process to verify your identity before investing.

Starting with mutual funds doesn't need a lot of money - just the right mindset, a small amount, and a plan you stick to

"It includes submitting proof of your ID and address" explained Ananya. *"Your Aadhaar and PAN card usually do the job".*

"For kids, it's done under a parent or guardian's name" added Zara.

Step 2: Choose a Platform

Aarav said, "There are many apps and websites where you can invest in mutual funds - like **Groww, Zerodha, Paytm Money**, or even through your bank".

"Make sure the platform is SEBI-registered and trustworthy" added Rohan.

"Most platforms let parents open minor accounts for kids too" said Ananya.

Step 3: Decide Your Investment Method

"You can invest in two ways" said Zara.

- **Lump Sum** - One-time investment of a bigger amount

- **SIP (Systematic Investment Plan)** - Regular investment of smaller amounts

"SIP is great for beginners" said Kabir. "It feels manageable".

"And it builds the saving habit" said Aarav.

Step 4: Choose the Fund

"Go back to what we learned" said Ananya. "Pick a fund based on:

- **Your goal**
- **Risk comfort**
- **Duration"**

"Use the fund factsheet to make your decision" said Zara.

"Start simple. Choose a fund with a solid track record" added Rohan.

Step 5: Start Investing

"Once you choose the fund, the app will show you the NAV and ask how much you want to invest" said Ananya.

"You can automate SIPs so they deduct money on a fixed date each month" said Aarav.

"And track your progress through the same app" added Zara.

Smart Tips for Beginners

Kabir asked, "Any tips before we start?"
Ananya smiled. "Always".

- *Start small and build confidence*
- *Stay consistent*
- *Avoid jumping between funds too often*
- *Don't panic during market dips*
- *Ask questions and keep learning*

Quick Recap

Zara summarised:

- KYC is the first step to start investing
- Choose a trusted platform
- Pick SIP or lump sum based on your situation
- Match your fund to your goal

- Automate and track your investments

"Next time" said Rohan, "we'll talk about the risks and myths - because understanding the downsides helps you grow smarter".

The Piggy Bank Society looked ready. They weren't just learning anymore - they were preparing to take action, one small investment at a time.

Chapter 6

Risks and Myths about Mutual Funds

When the Piggy Bank Society arrived at the library, Ananya had drawn two columns on the board. One said **"Risk"** and the other said **"Myth"**. Below them were sticky notes with phrases like "You can lose all your money" and "Guaranteed returns".

Kabir read them aloud. "These sound scary".

"They're not all true" said Zara. "Let's separate fact from fiction".

Myth 1: Mutual Funds Are Only for Experts

Rohan said, "Many people believe that mutual funds are too complex for regular folks".

"But we're just kids and we're already learning" said Aarav.

Mutual funds don't guarantee returns and they aren't only for the rich. The truth? They're for anyone willing to learn, plan, and accept the ride

"That's the point" said Ananya. *"Mutual funds are made for everyone - especially beginners. You don't need to know everything. The fund manager handles that".*

Myth 2: Guaranteed Returns

Zara read one note. "Mutual funds will double your money in 3 years".

"That's a myth" said Rohan. *"There's no guarantee. Returns depend on market performance".*

"Think of it like farming" said Ananya. "You can plant the seeds, but weather affects the outcome".

Risk 1: Market Ups and Downs

Aarav wrote:

Risk = The chance that your investment could go down in value.

"Equity funds go up and down with the stock market" he said.

"But over time, markets usually rise" said Rohan. "So long-term investors often benefit".

"Don't check your funds every day. Think big picture" said Zara.

Myth 3: You Need a Lot of Money to Start

Kabir asked, "Can I really start with ₹500?"

"Yes" said Ananya. "That's why SIPs exist. You can begin small and build steadily".

"It's not about how much you start with. It's about how long you stay invested" said Aarav.

Risk 2: Choosing the Wrong Fund

"Sometimes people pick funds just because they saw an ad or heard a tip" said Rohan.

"That's risky" said Zara. "You should choose based on your goal, not someone else's advice".

"Do your own research or talk to someone you trust" added Ananya.

Myth 4: Mutual Funds Are Like Fixed Deposits

"Wrong again" said Aarav. "FDs give fixed interest. Mutual fund returns can change".

"But they also have the potential to grow faster than FDs" said Rohan.

"They're different tools for different needs" said Ananya.

Quick Recap

Zara summarised:

- Mutual funds are beginner-friendly
- Returns are not guaranteed
- Markets can go up and down, so stay invested long-term
- You can start small with SIPs
- Avoid picking funds without research
- Mutual funds are not the same as fixed deposits

The Piggy Bank Society left that day feeling smarter. Busting myths had made mutual funds feel a lot less scary and a lot more exciting.

Chapter 7

Setting Goals with Mutual Funds

The library felt extra cozy that afternoon. Ananya had brought a stack of goal cards. Each one had a dream written on it - "Buy a laptop," "Go on a school trip to Goa," "Start a bakery," "Pay for college."

She spread them on the table.

"Today" she said, "we match dreams with funds".

Kabir picked up the bakery card. "That's totally mine".

Zara chose the laptop. "Let's learn how mutual funds can help us make these happen".

When you plant a goal and water it with discipline, time, and monthly SIPs, it grows into something real. Long-term dreams need long-term care

Step 1: Define Your Goal

Rohan said, "Before choosing a fund, you need to know why you're investing".

"Short-term goals are for things you need in a few months or a year" said Ananya. "Like a school trip or a bicycle".

"Long-term goals take years - like college or starting a business" added Aarav.

Kabir asked, "What about saving for both?"

"You can set up two different SIPs for each goal" said Zara. "It's all about being clear".

Step 2: Match the Right Fund to the Goal

Ananya explained:
- **Short-term goals** = *Safer funds like debt or short-term hybrid funds*
- **Long-term goals** = *Equity funds for higher growth*

"If you're going to use the money soon, choose safety. If you've got time, go for growth" said Rohan.

Step 3: Decide How Much to Invest

Aarav said, "Figure out how much your goal costs and how much time you have".

"If a laptop costs ₹30,000 and you want it in 2 years, you'll need to invest about ₹1,200 per month in a SIP" said Zara.

"That way, you don't need a huge amount all at once" said Ananya. "You grow into your goal".

Step 4: Track Your Progress

"Every month, check your SIP progress" said Rohan. "It feels amazing to see how close you're getting".

"Celebrate small wins" said Kabir. "Like when you cross 25 percent of your goal".

"You can even create a goal tracker chart" suggested Aarav. "Make it visual".

Step 5: Stick With It

Zara said, "Sometimes the market will drop and your fund value might fall. Don't panic".

"Stick to your plan" said Ananya. *"The market goes up and down, but your goal stays steady"*.

"It's like training for a marathon" said Rohan. "You keep going, even if one day is tough".

Quick Recap

Ananya summarised:

- Set clear short-term and long-term goals
- Choose funds based on time and risk
- Calculate monthly SIPs to reach your goal
- Track your progress and celebrate milestones
- Stay consistent even when the market moves

"Next time" said Zara, "we'll see if we're truly ready - with a checklist and quiz to test what we've learned".

The Piggy Bank Society looked at their chosen cards again. Now they didn't feel like distant dreams. They felt like real, achievable goals - one SIP at a time.

Chapter 8

Are You Fund-Ready?

The Piggy Bank Society walked into the library for their final session on mutual funds. On the table were printed quizzes, stickers that read "Future Investor" and a giant checklist titled "Fund-Ready Scorecard".

"Today" said Ananya, "we see how much we've learned - and if we're ready to start our journey as investors".

Kabir picked up a quiz sheet. "Do we get prizes?"

"Only if you score more than 5 out of 7" winked Zara.

Being fund-ready isn't about having a lot of money. It's about having the mindset - understanding risk, staying consistent, and thinking long-term.

Quiz Time: Are You Paying Attention?

Rohan read aloud:

- What does NAV stand for?
- What is a SIP?
- Which fund is safest for short-term goals?
- Who manages your investments in a mutual fund?
- True or False: Mutual funds always give guaranteed returns.
- What is one thing you should track regularly in a fund?
- What does diversification mean?

Everyone scribbled their answers. They checked with each other and tallied their scores.

"6 out of 7!" shouted Kabir.

"Future Investor sticker for you" said Ananya.

The Fund-Ready Checklist

Ananya held up the big checklist:

- I know what a mutual fund is
- I understand SIP and NAV
- I know the three main types of funds
- I can choose a fund based on my goal

- I know how to start investing with a parent's help
- I'm not expecting magic money or overnight success

"If you can tick at least five boxes" said Zara, "you're fund-ready".

Tips for the Road Ahead

Aarav said, "Even after this, keep reading and asking questions".

"Markets change, but learning never stops" said Rohan.

"Also, talk to your parents" said Ananya. "Ask them about the funds they invest in".

"You could even suggest starting a family SIP for your future goals" said Zara.

Dream Big, Start Small

Kabir looked at his quiz sheet and smiled. "I never thought I'd understand mutual funds. Now I actually feel excited".

"Money is not just something you spend" said Ananya. "It's something you can grow".

"And now you know how" said Rohan.

Quick Recap

Zara summarised:
- Mutual funds are team investments managed by experts
- SIPs make it easy to invest regularly
- Choosing the right fund depends on your goal and time frame
- Stay patient and consistent
- Keep learning and involve your family

The Piggy Bank Society high-fived each other. They had turned mutual fund learning into a fun, doable journey - one that would continue long after this book ended.

They weren't just students anymore. They were investors in training.

MONEY PSYCHOLOGY

Chapter 1

Why We Spend Even When We Don't Need To

It was a regular school day, and the Piggy Bank Society was hanging out in the library after lunch. Zara walked in holding a shopping bag.

"Guess what? I went to buy a notebook and ended up with this fancy water bottle, a pack of neon pens, and a sticker set".

Kabir looked inside the bag and laughed. "So... none of that was on your list?"

"Nope" said Zara. "I don't even like neon pens. They just looked cool in the store".

Ananya smiled. "Perfect timing. Today, we're starting a new topic - how our minds play games with our money".

Sometimes, it's not the wallet that makes the decision - it's the feeling in the moment. Our brain loves rewards, even when we don't need them

What Is Impulse Buying?

Rohan wrote on the board:

Impulse Buying = Buying something without planning, just because it looks tempting.

"It's when you buy something just because you feel like it - not because you really need it" said Ananya.

Kabir nodded. "Like that giant lollipop I bought last week and didn't even finish".

"Exactly" said Zara. "And the strange thing is, most of us do it, even when we know better".

----- ◆ -----

Emotion vs. Logic

Aarav explained, "Our brain is split into two teams when it comes to money:

- The Emotion Team: loves fun, reacts quickly, wants rewards now
- The Logic Team: thinks about consequences, future plans, and long-term goals"

"When you're excited, tired, or even bored, the Emotion Team takes over" said Rohan.

"That's why people buy things just because they're on sale or look good" added Zara.

The Brain's Reward Button

Ananya said, "Our brain has something called **dopamine** - *a feel-good chemical.* We get a shot of it when we buy something new".

"Even if we don't need it?" asked Kabir.

"Yup. That's why shopping can feel exciting, even when it makes no sense" said Zara.

"And it's not just shopping. Likes on social media, eating junk food, winning a game - all trigger dopamine" said Aarav.

Why Stores Know More About You Than You Think

Rohan showed a slide of a supermarket layout. "Ever noticed chocolates and chips are always near the billing counter?"

"That's called a **trigger spot**" said Ananya. "It's designed to tempt you while you wait".

"*Bright colours, flashy signs, words like 'limited edition'* - all of it is to get your Emotion Team excited" said Zara.

Real-Life Traps

Kabir shared, "Last week I saw a flash sale on an online game. I didn't even check the price. Just clicked 'Buy Now'".

"That's the **power of urgency**" said Aarav. "It makes you feel like you'll miss out if you wait".

"It's called **FOMO - Fear of Missing Out**" said Rohan. "One of the strongest money traps".

Quick Fixes

Zara suggested, "Here's how to beat the impulse:

- Make a list before you shop
- Wait 24 hours before buying non-essential stuff
- Ask: *'Do I need this or just want it because it's shiny?'*"

Ananya added, "And avoid shopping when you're tired, hungry, or stressed. That's when the Emotion Team wins easily".

Quick Recap

Rohan wrapped up:
- Impulse buying is spending without planning
- Our brains chase rewards, not logic
- Stores and apps are designed to trigger spending
- You can fight back by slowing down and staying aware

"Next time" said Zara, "we'll dive deeper into how ads, influencers, and brands get into our heads - and sometimes even into our wallets".

The Piggy Bank Society walked out a little more mindful. The next time they felt that urge to buy something sparkly, they had a secret weapon - awareness.

Chapter 2

The Tricks Behind
Ads and Influencers

The next meeting began with a little game. Zara handed everyone a blank piece of paper and said, "Write down the first three ads you remember seeing today".

Within seconds, the sheets were filled.

"Wow" said Kabir. "I didn't realise I saw that many ads before lunch".

"That's the point" said Ananya. "They're everywhere. And they're designed to sneak into your brain".

What Makes Ads So Powerful?

Rohan stood up and drew three circles:

- **Attention** - Grab your focus quickly
- **Emotion** - Make you feel something
- **Action** - Make you want to do or buy something

*Sometimes we buy things not because we need them…
but because someone on a screen made it look impossible
to resist*

"Good ads don't just show you a product" he said. "They tell you a story".

"Sometimes a story so good, you don't even realise it's trying to sell you something" added Zara.

The Tricks Ads Use

Ananya listed some common tactics:

- **Celebrities and Influencers** - You trust them, so you trust the product
- **Social Proof** - "1 million people bought this" makes it feel safe to buy
- **FOMO** - Limited-time deals or flash sales create urgency
- **Aspirational Messaging** - "Buy this and be cooler, smarter, faster"
- **Repetition** - See something enough times and it starts to feel familiar and trustworthy

"They aren't lying" said Rohan. "But they're definitely guiding how you feel".

The Science of Design

Aarav showed two images of water bottles - one plain, one brightly coloured with a cartoon character.

"Which one would you pick?" he asked.

"Cartoon one, obviously" said Kabir.

"That's the power of design" said Ananya. *"Colour, fonts, packaging - all influence what we think looks better or 'cooler.'"*

"And jingles too" said Zara. "If you can hum it, you'll remember it. That's why ad tunes are so catchy".

Influencers and Hidden Promotions

Kabir asked, "What about YouTubers? Are they part of advertising too?"

"Definitely" said Rohan. "Many get paid to talk about products. It's called **sponsored content**".

"But sometimes, they don't even tell you it's an ad" said Aarav.

"That's why you need to ask yourself - are they sharing because they love it, or because they're paid to?" said Zara.

Ads That Make You Feel Less

Ananya said, "Some ads are sneaky. They make you feel not good enough - unless you buy their product".

"That's called **insecurity marketing**" said Rohan. "It plays on your fears".

"You're not tall enough, smart enough, cool enough - until you buy their shampoo or shoes" added Zara.

"But you're already enough" said Aarav. "A product can't change that".

How to Outsmart Ads

Ananya gave a few tips:

- **Ask yourself:** *Do I want this, or do I just want to feel what the ad is showing?*
- Look for real reviews, not just shiny ones
- Be aware of how things are presented - not just what is said
- Wait before buying something you saw in an ad

"Even just noticing the trick makes you stronger" said Rohan.

Quick Recap

Zara wrapped up:

- Ads use attention, emotion, and action to influence you
- Celebrity, design, and urgency tricks are everywhere
- Influencers are part of the marketing world
- Not all ads are honest - some play on your fears
- Awareness is the best way to resist being tricked

"Next time" said Ananya, "we'll switch sides and ask - why is saving so difficult, even when we know it's good for us?"

The Piggy Bank Society packed up their notebooks, ready to face the next video, billboard, or social post - not with wide eyes, but with wise ones.

Chapter 3

What Makes Us Save (or Not Save)?

The room was unusually quiet when the Piggy Bank Society met again. Rohan placed two small chocolate bars on the table and said, "Okay, who wants one now - or two if you can wait for 15 minutes?"

Kabir's hand shot up. "One now, please!"

Ananya laughed. "This is called the **Marshmallow Test.** It's a famous experiment where kids were tested to see if they could wait for a bigger reward later".

"And it tells us a lot about how we think about saving" added Zara.

Why Is Saving So Hard?

Rohan wrote on the board:

Saving = Choosing long-term goals over short-term fun.

Some of us save for something bigger. Others spend for something immediate. The difference often isn't money - it's mindset

"That's not always easy" he said. "Our brains are wired to want rewards now".

Kabir said, "It's like wanting to buy a new cricket bat today instead of saving for a better one later".

"Exactly" said Aarav. "That urge to spend now is strong".

The Role of Dopamine

Ananya explained, "Remember dopamine? The chemical that makes you feel good?"

"When you buy something or eat something tasty, your brain releases dopamine" said Zara.

"Saving doesn't give the same instant excitement. That's why it's harder" added Rohan.

"But small wins can help. Like seeing your piggy bank fill up or watching your savings goal get closer" said Aarav.

Saving Needs a Story

Kabir asked, "How do I get excited about saving?"

"Give your saving a purpose" said Zara. "Don't just say 'I'll save money.' Say 'I'm saving for that bicycle I want.'"

"Create a vision board or draw what you're saving for" said Ananya. "That makes it feel real".

Automatic vs. Manual

Rohan said, "Grown-ups use auto-debit to save without thinking. Kids can do something similar".

"Like putting ₹10 from every pocket money into a jar right away" suggested Aarav.

"Make it a habit, not a decision" said Zara.

Why Some People Save Less

Ananya explained, "Some people grow up in homes where saving isn't common. Or they've never seen anyone plan for the future".

"And sometimes, people are just struggling to meet daily needs" said Rohan. "Saving feels like a luxury".

"That's why even small savings matter. They build confidence" added Zara.

Games That Help You Save

Kabir said, "I once made a deal with myself. Every time I said no to a snack I didn't really need, I added ₹10 to my 'cool savings' box".

"That's brilliant" said Ananya. "Gamifying saving makes it fun".

"Turn it into a challenge with friends" said Aarav. "Who can save the most in a month?"

Quick Recap

Rohan wrapped up:

- Saving is hard because our brain loves instant rewards
- Dopamine makes spending exciting, but saving needs goals
- Give your savings a story or purpose
- Build habits that make saving automatic
- Make saving fun with games and mini rewards

The Piggy Bank Society left the library a little more determined. Saving wasn't boring anymore. It was a game, a plan, and a promise to their future selves.

Chapter 4

Investing and Risk – What Our Brain Thinks vs. What Actually Works

The Piggy Bank Society walked into the library to find a small plant on the table.

"Meet our new friend" said Ananya. "We'll water it every week. By the end of the term, let's see how it grows".

Kabir tilted his head. "Is this a gardening club now?"

"Nope" said Zara. "This is about investing - and how it's like growing a plant".

What Is Investing?

Rohan wrote on the board:

Investing = Putting money into something now so it grows over time.

When it comes to investing, our brains love thrill. But real success? That comes from balance, patience, and a plan

"Like buying a stock, mutual fund, gold, or even starting a small business" he explained.

"Or like buying good soil and watering this plant" added Aarav. "You don't get fruit tomorrow, but you get something better later".

Why the Brain Struggles with Risk

Zara said, "Our brains are not naturally good with risk. We like certainty".

"Spending money now feels safe. Investing feels risky, because we don't know exactly what we'll get or when" said Ananya.

"Even grown-ups panic when prices fall" said Rohan. "They want to sell quickly, even if that means a loss".

"It's called **loss aversion** - we hate losing more than we enjoy gaining" added Aarav.

Plant vs. Instant Noodles

Kabir laughed. "So investing is the plant. Spending is the instant noodles".

"Perfect example" said Zara. *"One takes patience. The other gives quick satisfaction"*.

"But only one lasts" said Rohan.

The Magic of Time

Ananya drew a graph on the board - a small curve that slowly rises. "This is what long-term investing looks like. The longer you wait, the more it grows".

"It's called **compound growth**" said Aarav. "Your money earns money. Then that money earns more money".

"Like a snowball rolling down a hill" added Rohan. "It starts small but builds big".

Safe vs. Risky Investments

Zara broke it down:

- **Safe**: Savings accounts, government bonds
- **Medium Risk**: Mutual funds, gold
- **High Risk**: Stocks, startups

"Everyone has a different risk comfort level" said Ananya. "You have to know your own".

"Start small, stay curious, and learn before you leap" said Aarav.

Thinking Long-Term

Kabir asked, "What if something goes wrong?"

"That's part of investing" said Rohan. "Not every seed grows. But if you plant enough and take care of them, most will".

"Don't panic if results are slow" said Zara. "Time is your best friend".

Quick Recap

Ananya summarised:

- Investing means planting money now for future growth
- The brain fears risk and prefers quick rewards
- Compound growth works best with patience
- Understand your risk level and start small
- Time and consistency matter more than chasing quick wins

The Piggy Bank Society looked at the little plant again. It hadn't changed. But somehow, they already knew it would.

Chapter 5

Behavioural Biases in Money Decisions

The next Piggy Bank Society session began with a fun challenge. Ananya wrote two questions on the board:

1. Would you rather get ₹50 today or ₹100 a month later?
2. If a shirt was ₹1,000 and is now ₹600, would you buy it - even if you don't need it?

Kabir grinned. "These are money traps, aren't they?"

"Yup" said Zara. "Welcome to the world of behavioural biases - the sneaky shortcuts our brains take when making money decisions".

We like to believe our choices are always smart but sometimes we're just following habits our brain has quietly built

What Are Behavioural Biases?

Rohan explained, "They're habits or patterns in our thinking that affect how we decide - often without us realising it".

"Our brains try to save energy by using shortcuts" said Ananya. "But sometimes, those shortcuts lead us the wrong way".

Common Money Biases (And How They Trick Us)

1. Anchoring Bias

Zara explained, "You see a t-shirt marked ₹2,000 but on sale for ₹999. Suddenly, it feels like a bargain".

"But was it really worth ₹2,000 in the first place?" asked Aarav.

"Our brain *'anchors'* to the first number it sees. So ₹999 feels cheap in comparison" said Rohan.

2. Herd Behaviour

Kabir said, "Like when everyone's buying the same cricket shoes, so I feel like I need them too".

"That's herd thinking" said Zara. "We follow others because it feels safer".

"But what's right for the crowd may not be right for you" said Ananya.

3. Loss Aversion

Aarav explained, "We hate losing more than we love winning. That's why people sell stocks in panic or never invest at all".

"It's better to avoid mistakes than chase gains - that's what our brain tells us" said Rohan.

"But that can stop us from taking smart risks" added Zara.

4. Sunk Cost Fallacy

Ananya asked, "Ever sat through a boring movie just because you paid for the ticket?"

"Totally" said Kabir.

"That's sunk cost thinking. We stick with bad choices because we've already spent money or time - even if quitting is smarter" said Aarav.

5. Confirmation Bias

Rohan said, "We look for information that supports what we already believe".

"If I think a brand is cool, I'll only notice the good reviews and ignore the bad ones" said Zara.

"That can blind us to better options" said Ananya.

How to Outsmart Your Biases

Aarav listed a few tips:

- Pause before big decisions
- **Ask yourself:** *Am I thinking emotionally or logically?*
- Get a second opinion
- Write down pros and cons
- Don't follow the crowd blindly

"Your brain is powerful" said Rohan. "But it needs a little coaching sometimes".

Quick Recap

Zara summarised:

- Behavioural biases are mental shortcuts that can affect money decisions
- Anchoring, herd behaviour, loss aversion, sunk cost, and confirmation bias are common traps
- Awareness and simple questions can help avoid bad choices

The Piggy Bank Society left the library feeling like detectives - ready to question their own brains before their next buy.

Chapter 6

Marketing Tricks to Get You to Buy More

The Piggy Bank Society entered the library to find the table covered with candy, juice boxes, notebooks, and signs that said things like "Buy One Get One Free" and "Limited Time Only".

"Are we setting up a store?" asked Kabir, grabbing a juice box.

"Not quite" said Zara. "Today we're talking about how shops and brands use clever tricks to make you spend more than you planned".

Ananya pointed to the signs. "These are some of the oldest tricks in the book - and they still work".

The Power of BOGO and Bundling

Rohan started, "**BOGO means Buy One Get One.** It sounds like you're getting something free".

Smart marketing isn't about what you need - it's about making you feel like you'll miss out if you don't act now

"But sometimes you only wanted one" said Aarav. "Now you're buying more than you needed".

"Bundling is when products are sold together - like shampoo and conditioner, or notebook plus stickers" said Zara.

"You feel like you're saving money, but you might be spending more" said Ananya.

The 99 Trick

Kabir picked up a sign that read ₹199.

"This one feels like ₹100 less than ₹200" he said.

"Exactly" said Rohan. "It's called **charm pricing**. ₹199 sounds cheaper than ₹200, even though it's just one rupee difference".

"Our brains focus on the first digit" said Aarav.

Limited Time Only!

Zara pointed to a big red label that read "Offer ends today!"

"Urgency is a big trick" she said. "It makes you feel like you'll miss out if you don't act now".

"That's FOMO again" said Kabir. **"Fear of Missing Out".**

"Shops know that urgency creates action" said Ananya.

Size and Packaging Tricks

Aarav held up two bags of chips. "One is bigger, but has less inside".

"That's **packaging psychology**" said Rohan. "Big bags, flashy colours, and words like 'jumbo' make you think you're getting more".

"Sometimes you're just paying for air" joked Kabir.

Loyalty Cards and Freebies

"Ever been offered a 'Buy 9, get the 10th free' card?" asked Zara.

"Yep" said Kabir. "I have a juice shop card like that".

"It's called a **loyalty program**" said Ananya. "It encourages you to come back more - and spend more - just to get the reward".

"And most people spend more than what that 'free' thing is worth" said Rohan.

How to Outsmart the Tricks
==========================

Ananya listed tips:

- Make a list before you shop - and stick to it
- **Ask yourself:** *Would I buy if there were no offer?*
- Compare prices per unit (like per gram or ml)
- Walk away and come back later - urgency fades

"The best shoppers are slow thinkers" said Aarav.

Quick Recap
===========

Zara summed it up:

- Marketing uses tricks like BOGO, bundling, charm pricing, and urgency
- Packaging and loyalty programs are designed to make you spend more
- Awareness helps you buy what you need, not just what's on offer

The Piggy Bank Society walked out of their pretend store a little wiser. The next time they saw a flashy offer, they would see it for what it really was - a nudge, not a necessity.

Chapter 7

Becoming a Conscious Consumer and Investor

The library was quieter than usual. The Piggy Bank Society had just watched a short documentary on how much plastic waste is generated from online shopping.

"I didn't think about what happens after I throw the packaging" said Kabir quietly.

Zara nodded. "It's not just about how much we spend. It's about what we spend on - and why".

Ananya picked up a marker and wrote two words on the board: **Conscious Choices.**

◆

What Is a Conscious Consumer?

Rohan explained, *"It means buying with awareness. You ask questions before spending".*

"Do I really need this? Who made it? Is it helping someone or hurting something?" added Aarav.

Being a mindful consumer means looking beyond flashy labels - it's about understanding what you buy, why you buy it, and how it impacts the world

"It's not about being perfect. It's about thinking before buying" said Zara.

Questions to Ask Before Buying

Ananya shared a checklist:

- Do I need this or just want it?
- Will I use it more than once?
- Is there a better quality version that lasts longer?
- Can I borrow it instead of buying?
- Does the product harm the environment?

"Every rupee you spend is like a vote" said Rohan. "It supports the kind of world you want to live in".

The Pressure to Fit In

Kabir asked, "But what if all my friends are buying the same thing? Like new shoes or the latest game?"

"That's real" said Zara. "Peer pressure is strong".

"But if you understand your own values, it gets easier to say no" said Aarav.

"Being different takes confidence. But that's what leaders do" said Ananya.

What Is a Conscious Investor?

Rohan explained, "*An investor puts money into companies, businesses, or ideas. A conscious investor looks beyond profit*".

"They ask - does this company treat its workers well? Is it polluting rivers? Does it support education?" said Zara.

"These are called **ESG factors - Environment, Social, and Governance**" said Aarav.

"You're not just growing your money. You're growing the future" said Ananya.

Choosing Value Over Hype

Kabir said, "Sometimes I buy things just because they're trending".

"That's normal" said Rohan. "But trends fade. Value lasts".

"If something helps you, lasts long, or supports a good cause - that's value" said Zara.

Small Steps That Matter

Ananya gave ideas:

- Choose reusable over single-use
- Support local sellers and ethical brands
- Ask more questions at stores
- Share or swap instead of buying
- Spend on experiences, not just things

"It's not about spending less" said Aarav. "It's about spending better".

Quick Recap

Zara wrapped up:

- Conscious consumers think before buying
- Peer pressure is strong, but personal values can guide you
- Conscious investors care about how companies act, not just how they earn
- Value lasts longer than trends
- Spending wisely helps the world and your wallet

The Piggy Bank Society left with a little more purpose in their steps. They weren't just money smart - they were money wise.

Chapter 8

Building a Strong Money Mindset

The final meeting of the Piggy Bank Society felt different. They had spent weeks learning about money, savings, investing, and the power of being smart with their choices. Today, Ananya had something even bigger to talk about - the money mindset.

"I was thinking" she said, "how do you feel about money? Does it excite you, stress you out, or make you want to avoid it?"

Kabir shrugged. "Money is cool... but sometimes, it just seems like something I'm always thinking about, but never getting enough of".

"That's exactly why we need a money mindset" said Zara. "It's the way you think about money that helps you stay calm, focused, and successful with it".

A strong money mindset isn't built in a day. It comes from small, thoughtful choices repeated often - with clarity, calm, and purpose

What Is a Money Mindset?

Rohan wrote on the board:

Money Mindset = Your attitude toward money and how you handle it.

"It's not just about saving or spending" said Ananya. "It's about your relationship with money. How you think about it, how you manage it, and how it affects your life".

"Some people see money as something to hoard and save" said Zara. "Others see it as something to spend quickly".

"And there are people who believe it can be used to build things and help others" added Aarav.

Growth Mindset vs. Fixed Mindset

Ananya introduced the idea of growth mindset. *"A growth mindset is believing you can get better at money management, just like anything else in life"*.

"By learning and practicing, you grow your money mindset" said Rohan.

"On the other hand, *a fixed mindset is when you think you can't change your money habits*" said Zara.

"Like when you believe you'll never be good at saving or investing".

"Both mindsets affect how you handle challenges and setbacks" added Ananya.

Money Mindset and Emotions

Kabir asked, "But what if I get upset about money? Like, when I don't have enough for something I really want?"

"Money can be emotional" said Zara. "That's why it's important to stay calm. If you don't have enough now, saving is the answer. It's okay to feel disappointed, but that's not a reason to panic".

"Your money mindset helps you stay balanced and calm" said Rohan. "If you think long-term, you know that you can work toward what you want".

Building Confidence with Money

Ananya smiled. "Building a strong money mindset starts with confidence. You believe in your ability to manage your money and make smart choices".

"Confidence doesn't mean never making mistakes" said Zara. *"It means being willing to learn from them and improve"*.

"Confidence also means knowing that there are resources - books, apps, and mentors - that can help you if you're unsure" added Rohan.

Setting Goals and Staying Focused

Aarav said, "The best way to grow your money mindset is by setting goals - big and small".

Ananya agreed, "Your goals help you stay focused. They give you something to work toward, whether it's saving for a gadget, a trip, or even starting your own business".

"The more you work toward your goals, the more you build confidence" said Rohan.

"Break big goals into small steps" said Zara. "A small goal might be saving ₹100 this week, while the big goal might be ₹1,000 in two months".

Learn from Mistakes
and Keep Going

Kabir smiled. "I guess it's not just about the money. It's about how I learn from my choices".

"Exactly" said Ananya. *"Building a money mindset isn't about perfection. It's about progress"*.

"Setbacks happen. Mistakes happen" said Zara. "But as long as you keep learning and improving, you're moving forward".

Quick Recap

Ananya wrapped up with the final thoughts:

- Money mindset is your attitude toward money and how you handle it
- Growth mindset means believing you can get better at managing money
- Stay calm, build confidence, and keep working toward your goals
- Learn from mistakes and make progress, not perfection

The Piggy Bank Society left the library with a new attitude toward money. Not as something to fear, but something to learn from and grow with. They were ready to face the world - one smart money decision at a time.

GOVERNMENT FINANCES

Chapter 1

Where Does the Government Get Its Money From?

It was the first meeting of the new term, and the Piggy Bank Society was back in action. The topic of the day? **Government money.** The room buzzed with excitement. Ananya stood at the whiteboard and wrote one big question:
"Where does the government get its money from?"

Kabir raised his hand instantly. "From the Prime Minister's wallet?"

Everyone laughed.

"Not quite" said Zara, smiling. "But the answer is actually quite interesting. And we're going to break it down today".

The government isn't a magician - it needs money just like everyone else. And that money comes from all of us, flowing in from many small streams to power the nation's big dreams

Public Money, Private Pockets

Rohan opened a notebook. "Think about everything the government does. Build roads, run schools, operate trains, provide water, manage hospitals. All of that needs money".

"So where does it come from?" asked Aarav.

"From all of us" said Ananya. "The government earns money through something called **taxes**".

"Wait. So when I buy a ₹10 packet of chips, the government earns something?" asked Kabir.

"Yes" said Zara. "There is tax included in the price. It may be small, but when you add it up across a billion people, it becomes big".

What Are Taxes?

Ananya explained, *"A tax is a small part of what you earn or spend that you give to the government. In return, they use that money to provide services"*.

Rohan drew a pie chart on the board. "The government earns money from different sources. Taxes are the biggest part".

Sources of government income:

- *Income Tax*
- *Goods and Services Tax (GST)*
- *Customs Duty (tax on imports)*
- *Excise Duty (on fuel, alcohol, etc.)*
- *Corporate Tax (paid by companies)*
- *Dividends from government companies*
- *Fees, fines, and more*

Who Decides What Gets Taxed?

"The government creates the rules" said Aarav. "The **Ministry of Finance** decides the tax rates every year".

"That's when the *Finance Minister presents the Union Budget in Parliament*" said Zara.

Kabir looked puzzled. "What's the **Union Budget?**"

"It's like a giant money plan" said Ananya. "We'll dive into that in the next chapter".

Quick Recap

Before they packed up, Zara summarised:

- The government needs money to run the country
- Most of it comes from taxes paid by people and businesses
- Even small purchases include taxes
- Paying taxes is how we contribute to better roads, schools, hospitals, and more

"In the next meeting" said Ananya, "we'll explore what happens to all that money. Who plans it, how they spend it, and how the budget is made".

The Piggy Bank Society left the room a little more curious. After all, their ₹10 chips were doing more than just satisfying hunger. They were building a country.

Chapter 2

What Is Tax and Why Do We Pay It?

The library was filled with the sound of rain tapping on the windows as the Piggy Bank Society gathered around. Zara had brought along a packet of biscuits and placed it in the center of the table.

"Guess how much tax I paid on this ₹20 packet?" she asked.

Kabir shrugged. "A rupee?"

"Close" said Zara. "But it proves a point. Even biscuits are taxed. And today we're going to learn why".

Tax isn't a punishment - it's a contribution. When we all pitch in, we build more than roads and buildings. We build community

What Is Tax, Really?

Ananya stood up and wrote a simple definition on the board:

Tax = A payment we make to the government to help run the country.

"It's not optional" she added. "It's a duty. But it also helps everyone, including us".

"So we're kind of co-owners of the country?" said Kabir.

"Exactly" said Rohan. "By paying tax, you're helping build roads, run schools, and fund hospitals".

Types of Taxes in Simple Words

Aarav created two big boxes on the board:

1. Direct Taxes:
- Paid directly by individuals or companies (Corporate Tax)
- *Example: Income Tax (paid on your salary or earnings)*
- Based on how much you earn

2. Indirect Taxes:
- Paid when you buy something
- Included in the price of goods or services

- *Example: GST (on food, clothes, gadgets, movie tickets)*

"You may not earn yet" said Zara, "but if you've ever bought a packet of chips or a video game, you've paid tax".

A Day in the Life of Tax

Rohan narrated a fun example:
- You take a cab to school – GST included
- You buy a chocolate bar – GST again
- Your parent pays income tax from their salary
- The school pays property tax

"Every part of your day is touched by taxes" said Ananya.

But Where Does It Go?

Kabir raised a good question. "If I pay ₹2 as tax, where does it actually go?"

"It goes into the **Consolidated Fund of India**" said Rohan. *"That's the main account the government uses to collect and spend money"*.

"And that money is used for public services" added Aarav. "Schools, highways, defense, sanitation, healthcare, you name it".

"So every taxpayer, even a kid buying a cookie, is funding the country's future" said Zara.

Common Misunderstandings

Ananya listed a few things people often get wrong:

- "I don't earn, so I don't need to know about taxes". *(Wrong. You still pay GST)*
- "Taxes are bad". *(No. They build our public life)*
- "Only rich people pay taxes". *(No. Everyone contributes, even in small ways)*

Tax and Responsibility

"Being a responsible citizen means more than voting" said Zara. "It means understanding how the country works".

"And taxes are at the heart of it" said Rohan.

Kabir smiled. "So I guess my biscuits just helped fix a road somewhere".

"Probably" said Ananya. "Or helped pay a teacher's salary".

Quick Recap

Zara noted the main takeaways:

- Tax is a payment to the government for running the country
- There are two main types: direct (like income tax) and indirect (like GST)
- We pay taxes in some way, even kids
- Tax money is used for roads, schools, hospitals, defense, and public services
- Knowing about taxes makes you a smarter citizen

"Next up" said Ananya, "we look at the government's biggest money event of the year. **The Union Budget**".

The Piggy Bank Society ended the session with a whole new respect for the word tax. It wasn't just about money. It was about belonging.

Chapter 3

Meet the Budget – The Country's Money Plan

The next Piggy Bank Society meeting kicked off with Aarav placing a stack of newspapers on the table. "These were all from Budget Day last year" he said. "Every headline talked about it".

"What's the big deal about the Union Budget?" asked Kabir.

"It's like the country's master plan for money" said Ananya. "And today, we're going to figure it out".

What Is the Union Budget?

Zara stood up and wrote on the board:

Union Budget = A plan made by the government every year on how to earn and spend money.

"It's presented by the Finance Minister in Parliament every year around Feb" she said.

Every country runs on choices. A budget isn't just math - it's a story of what matters most. Behind every coin is a decision

"And it affects everything" added Rohan. "From fuel prices to how many new schools are built".

Income vs. Expenditure

Ananya drew two boxes:

Revenue (Income):
- Taxes (income tax, GST, customs)
- Non-tax revenue (fees, fines, dividends from PSUs)

Expenditure (Spending):
- Education and healthcare
- Roads, railways, airports
- Defence and security
- Subsidies and welfare programs

"Imagine running a big household" said Aarav. "You have to plan what's coming in and where it's going".

What's in the Budget?

Rohan listed some common terms:

- **Fiscal Deficit** – When spending is more than earnings
- **Capital Expenditure** – Money spent on building assets like roads, bridges

- **Revenue Expenditure** – Day-to-day running costs like salaries and pensions

"The goal is to balance needs and growth" said Zara.

Budget and You

Kabir looked confused. "But I'm a student. How does the budget affect me?"

"Good question" said Ananya. "Here's how:
- If the education budget goes up, schools may get better facilities
- If GST on laptops is reduced, they become cheaper
- If public transport is improved, your commute is easier
- If scholarships are increased, more kids can study"

"So it affects every part of our lives" said Rohan.

How the Budget Is Made

Aarav explained the process:
- Ministries estimate how much money they'll need
- The Finance Ministry collects this information

- They plan how much money the government will earn and spend
- The budget is presented and debated in Parliament

"And after approval, it becomes the official plan" said Zara.

Real Examples from Previous Budgets

Ananya shared a few:

- *Digital India push* – More computer labs in schools
- *Health allocation increase* – New AIIMS hospitals being set up
- *Tax rebates* – Salaried people saving more money
- *PM Gati Shakti* – New infrastructure projects announced

"These are not just numbers" said Rohan. "They are decisions that shape lives".

Quick Recap

Zara summarised:

- The Union Budget is the government's yearly plan for earning and spending money
- It includes everything from schools to highways, from taxes to pensions
- It is presented by the Finance Minister in Parliament
- It directly affects citizens, including students and families

"In the next chapter" said Ananya, "we'll look closely at how this money is spent-and how every rupee is tracked".

The Piggy Bank Society left the library with a new sense of importance. The budget wasn't boring anymore. It was powerful.

Chapter 4

How the Government Spends Our Money

The rain had cleared up by the next Piggy Bank Society meeting, and the air felt fresh. Zara brought along a printout that looked like a colourful pie chart.

"This is last year's Union Budget spending breakdown" she said. "Want to see where our taxes go?"

Kabir leaned in. "Please tell me at least some of it goes to pizza".

"No pizza" said Ananya, laughing. "But definitely roads, railways, schools, and hospitals".

Big Buckets of Spending

Rohan explained the main sectors:

- **Education** – *Building schools, teacher salaries, mid-day meals, scholarships*
- **Healthcare** – *Hospitals, health missions, vaccination programs*

Every rupee the government spends travels a path - to build hospitals, fix roads, or educate children. Knowing where your money goes is the first step to becoming a thoughtful citizen

- **Infrastructure** – *Roads, highways, railways, airports*
- **Defence** – *Army, Navy, Air Force, border security*
- **Agriculture** – *Support for farmers, irrigation, crop insurance*
- **Welfare Schemes** – *Subsidies for gas, food, pensions for the elderly*

"The budget is like a plate" said Zara. "And each sector gets a slice".

Case Study: Mid-Day Meals

Ananya pulled out a photo of a school lunch being served.

"The Mid-Day Meal Scheme provides free lunch to students in government schools" she said. "It encourages kids to attend school and improves nutrition".

"And this is paid for by the government?" asked Kabir.

"Yes" said Rohan. "Money for it comes from the education and food welfare budgets".

How Spending Is Decided

Aarav explained:

- Ministries send proposals to the Finance Ministry
- Priorities are based on public needs and national goals
- Money is allocated according to urgency and impact

"So if a village has no electricity" said Zara, "it might get a new power project in that year's budget".

What About Freebies?

Kabir asked, "Sometimes I hear people talk about freebies. Are they wasteful?"

"It depends" said Ananya. *"Free school meals, free health checkups, or free gas connections may seem like freebies but they help improve lives".*

"The goal is to create equal opportunities" added Rohan. "So people can grow, work, and contribute back to the economy".

Tracking Government Spending

Zara shared a cool fact. "The government has websites and dashboards where anyone can check how money is spent".

Ananya added, "This is called transparency. Citizens can see where their tax money goes".

"That makes the government more accountable" said Aarav.

Balancing Priorities

"Spending is not unlimited" said Rohan. "The government has to choose".

"More on roads might mean less on health. More on defence might mean less on education" said Zara.

"Just like a family budget" said Ananya. "You cannot buy everything at once. You plan".

Quick Recap

Before wrapping up, Aarav listed the key points:
- Government spending covers education, health, defence, welfare, infrastructure, and more
- Spending priorities are based on national needs
- Welfare schemes are not freebies but investments in people
- Citizens can track spending through online tools
- The budget is a balancing act, not a blank cheque

"In the next chapter" said Zara, "we'll look at one of the most common taxes in India and how it affects everything from your pencil box to your sneakers".

The Piggy Bank Society ended the session with a new view of how their country worked. Behind every classroom light, road sign, or bridge, there was a budget that made it happen.

Chapter 5

The Big Role of GST and Indirect Taxes

The next time the Piggy Bank Society met, Rohan arrived with a shopping bag full of small items - a chocolate bar, a soft drink can, a packet of pens, and a receipt.

"Guess what all these have in common?" he asked.

"They're all snacks?" said Kabir.

"They all include GST" said Zara. "Even if we don't see it, we're paying tax on almost everything we buy".

What Is GST?

Ananya wrote on the board:

GST = Goods and Services Tax

Not all taxes are seen but they're always there. From your shampoo bottle to a chocolate bar, GST tags along, quietly building the nation's roads, bridges, and dreams.

"It's a type of indirect tax" she explained. "It's charged when you buy goods (like clothes) or services (like a haircut or an online subscription)".

"Before GST, there were many different taxes - VAT, excise, service tax" said Aarav. "GST replaced all of them".

"And now it's one tax for the whole country" added Rohan. "That's why they call it **One Nation, One Tax**".

GST in Daily Life

Zara pulled out the receipt. "This soft drink cost ₹30, but ₹3.60 of that was GST".

Kabir looked shocked. "So I pay tax even when I'm just thirsty?"

"Yep" said Ananya. "And the money goes to the government, not the shopkeeper".

Different GST Slabs

Aarav drew a simple chart:

- 0% – *Essential items (milk, fresh vegetables, rice)*
- 5% – *Some packaged foods, public transport*
- 12% – *Processed food, school bags*

- 18% – *Electronics, services like movie tickets*
- 28% – *Luxury goods (cars, air conditioners)*

"So the more luxurious the item, the higher the tax" said Rohan.

"Which is fair" added Zara. "It's called **progressive taxation**".

Who Collects GST?

Ananya explained, "Both the Central Government and State Governments share GST. That's why it's split into:

- *CGST (Central Goods and Services Tax)*
- *SGST (State Goods and Services Tax)*
- *IGST (Interstate GST - when goods move from one state to another)*

Kabir grinned. "So even a packet of chips can travel across tax systems".

GST for Businesses

Rohan added, "If you run a business, you collect GST from your customers and pay it to the government".

"And if your business earns above a certain limit, you must register for GST" said Ananya.

"Even online sellers and tutors who earn through platforms may need to pay" added Zara.

Why GST Matters

"GST has made tax collection easier, reduced corruption, and improved compliance" said Aarav.

"It also makes pricing transparent" said Rohan. "You know what part of your money is going where".

"And it helps the government plan better" said Zara. "They can estimate revenue more accurately".

Quick Recap

Before closing, Ananya summarised:

- GST is a unified indirect tax on goods and services
- It replaced multiple older taxes
- It affects most of our purchases
- Different items have different tax rates (slabs)
- Businesses must register for GST and collect it

"Next up" said Rohan, "we'll talk about something we don't pay yet, but will someday - income tax and the PAN card".

The Piggy Bank Society packed their things, amazed at how every packet of chips, can of cola, or trip to the mall played a role in building the nation's budget.

Chapter 6

Income Tax, PAN Cards, and Grown-Up Money

It was a bright Tuesday morning when the Piggy Bank Society gathered in the library. Kabir walked in looking very serious.

"My dad spent the whole weekend complaining about taxes" he said. "He mentioned something about income tax and this thing called a **PAN card**".

"Then today's your lucky day" said Ananya. "Because we're going to decode grown-up taxes".

What Is Income Tax?

Rohan wrote on the board:

Income Tax = A tax you pay on the money you earn.

"This is a direct tax" he explained. "You pay it directly to the government if you earn above a certain limit".

Grown-up money isn't just about earning more - it's about learning where it goes, what's deducted, and why it matters. Every paycheck tells a story of responsibility

"So only adults pay this?" asked Kabir.

"Yes" said Zara. "You only pay when you start earning money - like from a salary, business, or rent".

Who Pays Income Tax in India?

Ananya broke it down:

- Salaried employees (teachers, engineers, office workers)
- Business owners and shopkeepers
- Freelancers and online creators
- Landlords who earn from rent

"Even YouTubers who earn money from ads can be taxed" said Aarav.

How Much Tax Do You Pay?

Rohan explained with simple slabs:

- ₹0 to ₹4 lakh – No tax
- ₹4 lakh to ₹8 lakh – 5%
- ₹8 lakh to ₹12 lakh – 10%
- ₹12 lakh to ₹16 lakh – 15%
- ₹16 lakh to ₹20 lakh – 20%
- ₹20 lakh to ₹24 lakh – 25%
- ₹24 lakh and above – 30%

"Slabs may change each year in the Budget" added Zara. "And there are deductions too".

What Are Deductions?

"Deductions help reduce the amount of income you pay tax on" said Ananya.

Common deductions:
- Investment in Public Provident Fund (PPF)
- Life and health insurance premiums
- Home loan interest
- Donations to charity

"So if you invest or save wisely, you pay less tax" said Rohan.

Meet the PAN Card

Zara held up a sample card. "This is a **Permanent Account Number (PAN)** card".

"Every taxpayer needs one" said Ananya. "It's like your financial identity".

"You use it when opening bank accounts, investing, buying property, and filing taxes" said Aarav.

"It's issued by the Income Tax Department" added Rohan.

Filing Tax Returns

Kabir asked, "What happens at the end of the year?"

"You file an **Income Tax Return (ITR)**" said Ananya. *"That means telling the government how much you earned and paid in taxes"*.

"If you paid more than required, you get a refund" said Zara. "If you paid less, you pay the balance".

"You can file it online" said Aarav. "There are portals and apps for it".

Why It Matters

"Income tax is one of the biggest sources of government revenue" said Rohan.

"It funds everything from public transport to defence" added Ananya.

"And it builds trust in the system" said Zara. "Paying tax honestly keeps the economy healthy".

Quick Recap

Before wrapping up, Aarav summarised:

- Income tax is paid on earnings by individuals and businesses
- Only people who earn above a certain amount pay it
- You can reduce your tax using deductions
- A PAN card is needed for financial transactions and tax filing
- Filing tax returns is an annual responsibility

"In the next chapter" said Rohan, "we'll see how the government juggles between different priorities - spending, saving, and borrowing - just like a family budget".

The Piggy Bank Society walked out that day imagining the future - one where they would file their own returns and proudly say, "We know how taxes work".

Chapter 7

How Governments Balance Needs and Wants

It was a quiet afternoon in the school library. The Piggy Bank Society was gathered around a whiteboard filled with numbers and arrows. Kabir was staring at it with a puzzled look.

"This looks like my mom's grocery list after a discount sale" he said.

"Close" said Ananya. "But this is how the government decides what to spend on, and what to save for".

"Welcome to the world of budgeting - where needs and wants don't always match".

Every budget is a balancing act between dreams and duties, sparkles and staples. Smart governments (and kids) learn to weigh their decisions with both heart and head

What Is a Fiscal Deficit?

Rohan wrote it clearly on the board:

Fiscal Deficit = When the government spends more than it earns.

"If the government's income is ₹100 but it needs ₹120 for various schemes, the deficit is ₹20" said Zara.

"Then how does it manage the extra ₹20?" asked Kabir.

"By borrowing" said Aarav. "From the public, banks, or even foreign countries".

Just Like a Family Budget

Ananya smiled. "Your family also does this. You plan your monthly spending based on how much you earn".

Kabir nodded. "So if we want to eat out more, we cut down on online shopping".

"Exactly" said Zara. "The government does the same. It must prioritise".

What Are the Priorities?

Rohan listed key areas:

- **Basic needs:** *food, health, education*
- **Development:** *infra, technology*
- **Safety**: *defence, disaster response*
- **Future goals:** *environment, digital access*

"But it can't do everything at once" said Ananya. "It must choose".

"Like building more schools vs. reducing fuel prices" added Aarav.

Good Debt vs. Bad Debt

Zara explained, "*If the government borrows to build a highway or train network, that's good debt. It creates jobs and boosts the economy*".

"*But if it borrows too much for daily expenses, and can't repay, that's bad debt*" said Rohan.

"Too much debt means less money for future plans" said Ananya.

Making Tough Choices

Kabir asked, "So who decides what to cut and what to spend on?"

"The Finance Ministry plans it" said Zara. "But the entire Parliament debates and approves the budget".

"Sometimes, public opinion and elections also affect choices" added Rohan.

Balancing Growth and Welfare

Ananya gave an example: "A new expressway is good for business and jobs, but if rural schools don't have toilets, it's not balanced".

"The best budgets do both" said Aarav. "Support people today and build for tomorrow".

"It's not easy" said Zara. "That's why it's a careful balancing act".

Quick Recap

Rohan summarised:
- The government doesn't always have enough money for everything
- A fiscal deficit happens when spending is more than earnings
- Borrowing is okay if it leads to future growth
- Like a family, the government must prioritise needs over wants
- Smart spending builds a stronger future

"In our final chapter" said Ananya, "we'll take a peek at how the Budget and taxes are changing with technology - and what the future looks like".

The Piggy Bank Society packed up, realising that running a country wasn't just about collecting money. It was about making the tough calls - wisely.

Chapter 8

The Budget of Tomorrow

The final meeting of the term felt a little bittersweet. The Piggy Bank Society had spent weeks learning how money moved through the veins of the country. Today, they were wrapping it up by peeking into the future.

"So what's next?" asked Kabir. "Will we have robots collecting taxes?"

"Maybe" said Zara. "But one thing is certain and that is technology changing everything, even the budget".

Digital Budgeting

Ananya began, "Today, most budget documents are digital. No more printing thousands of pages".

"People can read it online, on apps, even in regional languages" said Rohan.

Tomorrow's budget isn't just numbers - it's a dream in the making. The future belongs to those who dare to imagine, plan, and build with purpose

"It's part of what we call transparency - everyone should be able to see how the country's money is being used" added Aarav.

AI and Data in Budget Planning

Zara explained, "The government now uses data and artificial intelligence to plan better".

"They can predict spending patterns, track tax payments, and even spot misuse faster" said Ananya.

"That makes decisions more accurate" said Rohan. "Less guesswork, more data".

Tracking Every Rupee

Kabir asked, "Can I actually see how my ₹2 chocolate tax is used?"

"Not directly" said Aarav. "But platforms like the *Public Financial Management System (PFMS)* let citizens track spending by ministry, district, or scheme".

"That builds trust" said Zara. "People feel part of the process".

Green Budgeting

"Another trend is green budgeting" said Ananya. *"This means planning with the environment in mind"*.

Rohan added, "Spending more on solar energy, electric buses, cleaning rivers, and disaster preparation".

"It's about long-term survival, not just quick results" said Aarav.

People's Budget and Feedback

Zara shared, "There are also pre-budget consultations, where farmers, students, businesses and citizens share ideas".

"So the budget is not just made by the government, but with the people" said Ananya.

"Imagine we submit ideas as the Piggy Bank Society" said Kabir.

"Why not?" said Rohan. "Citizen voices matter".

The Dream Budget

The group created their own wish list:

- Clean water in every school
- Financial literacy classes from Class 5
- Free Wi-Fi in government libraries
- Solar panels on all school rooftops

"These ideas may sound small" said Zara, "but every good budget starts with a big dream".

Quick Recap

Before leaving, Ananya summarised:

- Budgets are going digital and more transparent
- AI and data are improving planning and decision-making
- Citizens can track spending and give feedback
- Green budgets focus on climate and sustainability
- The best budgets are those that include everyone's voice

As they packed their things, Aarav smiled. "We started with chips and taxes. Now we're ending with AI and solar panels".

Kabir laughed. "Next stop - presenting our own budget someday".

And with that, The Piggy Bank Society wrapped up another powerful journey, proving once again that understanding money is not just for grown-ups - it's for every future leader.

Dear Reader,

You have just taken a big step by joining us on this financial adventure with The Piggy Bank Society and we are so proud of you! But remember, learning about money isn't something you finish in one book… **it's a journey that lasts your whole life.**

The best part? You don't have to walk this path alone. *Your parents, teachers, and even your own experiences are amazing teachers.* Ask questions. Notice how money is used at home, in shops, at school, or even online. **Every moment is a chance to learn how to make smarter choices.**

And here's something extra special: *Why not create your very own Piggy Bank Society with your friends?* Meet once a month, pick a topic (like savings, apps, or starting a tiny business), and talk about what you've learned. You will be amazed at how much fun learning about money can be when you do it together!

We'd also love it if you became a Piggy Bank Champion - share what you've learned with your classmates, cousins, neighbours… in fact anyone! You never know who you might inspire.

Thanks for being a part of this journey. The world needs more smart, kind, money-wise individuals like you.

See you in the next book!

About the Author

Charith Appachu is passionate about making finance simple, relatable, and exciting for young minds. With a strong belief that **financial literacy is a life skill** and not an optional subject, he is on a mission to help more students build confidence with money from an early age.

He brings decades of professional experience from leading global institutions such as **Deloitte** and **Goldman Sachs**, along with a PGDM from **SPJIMR**, one of India's top business schools. Combining real-world expertise with a deep interest in education, Charith regularly conducts **Finance Masterclass Programs** for teenagers, helping them understand money, markets, and decision-making in a way that sparks curiosity and confidence. Reach out to know more...

The Piggy Bank Society is a step towards making finance more accessible to young readers. If you found the book valuable, **it is also available on Amazon and Flipkart, and your positive review would go a long way in helping more students discover it.**

You can reach out to him at **charith@seed-edu.com**